Pumpkin Pie.

2 cups stewed and strained pumpkin.
2 cups rich milk or cream.
2 cups brown or granulated sugar.
2 eggs
½ teaspoon ginger
1 teaspoon salt
1 teaspoon cinnamon

Mix pumpkin with milk, sugar, beaten eggs, ginger, cinnamon, and beat 2 minutes. Pour into pie tin which has been lined with pastry. Place in hot oven for

(over)

THE
HEIRLOOMED
Kitchen

Made-from-Scratch Recipes
to Gather Around for Generations

ASHLEY SCHOENITH

Photography by Heidi Harris

Gibbs Smith

I'd like to dedicate this book to my family,
who inspire all that I do.

To my grandmother who inspired the past,
to Shane and to my parents who are such a gift in the present, and
to our children Wyatt, Sawyer, and Waylon who are the future.

————————

First Edition
28 27 26 25 24   5 4 3 2 1

Published by
Gibbs Smith
P.O. Box 667
Layton, Utah 84041

1.800.835.4993 orders
www.gibbs-smith.com

Designed by Rita Sowins | Sowins Design
Production Design by Renee Bond
Printed and bound in China
Gibbs Smith books are printed on either recycled, 100% post-consumer waste,
FSC-certified papers or on paper produced from sustainable PEFC-
certified forest/controlled wood source. Learn more at www.pefc.org.

Library of Congress Control Number: 2023941263
ISBN: 978-1-4236-6548-9

CONTENTS

Nana's Pie Crust

s flour
Crisco
salt
water

flour, salt & shortening w/
stir in water and turn into
shape in ball and set

in refrigerator for 15 min.

Turn into floured board and
roll.

Makes 2 9" shells or
1 top & bottom shell

INTRODUCTION

Find something you're passionate about and keep
tremendously interested in it.

—JULIA CHILD

Growing up, food was always made from scratch. We all sat down together as a family at the table for dinner. We were expected to "clean our plate" without complaint. I can remember many a night sitting at the table, pouting in protest, staring at my plate with a small pile of cooked lima beans from our garden until I finally choked them down. I also remember that every birthday cake was homemade and every Sunday had a pot roast in the oven or a big pot of spaghetti simmering on low. I recall rolling out sugar-cookie dough and decorating cookies for every holiday from the Fourth of July to Christmas using the same recipe from a falling-apart book on my mother's cookbook shelf in the pantry. The memories we make with food entangle all of our senses and they are lasting.

Now it's my turn to make food from scratch for my children. I am married to my husband, Shane, and we have three wonderful children, Wyatt, Sawyer, and Waylon. My family is my *why*—and by family, I mean those past and present. I like to think that my brand, Heirloomed, is a natural extension of both how I was raised and how we are raising our family today. It is my hope that it will also be how our kids one day raise their kids too. I like keeping things traditional and old-school, but I also acknowledge the need to adapt to a modern way of living as well.

For example, there are some old-school techniques and ingredients you may find as you work your way through this book. Recipes laden with lard or butter, because that's the way I learned to make them growing up and from following the recipe cards left to me by past generations. Do we eat this way every day? No. We choose to make these treasures for special occasions and on rotation with other healthy or more contemporary methods. However, you can bet your bottom dollar when a Sunday comes around that calls for biscuits, I'm making them from scratch the good old-fashioned way—with the lard and butter in all their glory.

My hope with this cookbook, and with all I do, is to pull from the past, to learn as much as I can, and to continue the story on for the next generation. If we don't make time to spend together with our mother or grandmother in the kitchen learning the tried-and-true family recipes we grew up on, then they'll be all but forgotten for future generations.

AN ODE TO THE FAMILY RECIPE

There is something to be said for a recipe itself. Given my line of business and a brand name like Heirloomed, I am often asked what is *my* most treasured family heirloom. It's hard to choose just one, but my answer is always the same: my stack of splattered family recipe cards, which were passed down to me from my great-grandmother (Nana) and grandmother's collections. Some are handwritten with notes, some were written on a typewriter, and the oldest are on brittle paper written in the most wonderful ink penmanship—all are treasures to me. I sift through them often, much like one would go through a stack of black-and-white photographs. I love reminiscing about the memories I have with some of these recipes and wondering how on earth others came to exist.

There is also something to be said about following a recipe, whether you're cooking something new from this cookbook or trying to follow an old family recipe card from your own collection. I often hear people say things like "it just doesn't taste the same as when Mom used to make it." There are so many reasons for that, nostalgia likely being the strongest. There is just something about someone else making something for you—made with love, if you will. Mastery of a recipe is not a science; it is truly an art form.

Baking is more of a science, in which measurements are important to obtain the right outcome, while cooking is more of a feeling, a balance of tasting and testing.

WHEN A RECIPE IS MORE THAN JUST A RECIPE

I'd like to challenge you to make time this year to visit family members who have inspired you in the kitchen, whomever they may be. Bring them blank recipe cards and ask them to handwrite a few of their signature recipes that you've enjoyed together so you can add them to your collection. Make time with them in the kitchen to make these favorite recipes step-by-step together and learn the nuances of the process itself. I can't tell you how many times I've asked someone, especially my older relatives, for a recipe and have been given the same answer, "Well, I don't have an actual recipe. A little of this, a dash of that . . ." Often they can't provide specifics on *how much* of something is needed because they've made it so many times and perfected it over the years. They know the desired outcome, what the consistency of the dough should be or how to make it come together without a second thought. It's a learned skill that's been perfected over the years, and one you should appreciate and learn.

This is why it is often hard to re-create Grandma's famous cookies or Mom's pot roast. You can follow a recipe to perfection, but if you haven't learned the techniques, consistencies, and subtle tips for mastering it, then the art will be lost and it will never be exactly the same again. I learn more from the scribbled notes on some of these old recipe cards than I do from the entire text of the recipe itself. "Make sure the water is *ice* cold," or "Do *not* overmix." The magic is in the process.

I say that, but truly where the magic lies is in the story. Some recipe notes were more interesting than helpful; for example, "From my neighbor, Doris Hart." It was "easy" to put together a cookbook full of recipes from a lifetime of cooking and baking in my own kitchen. We cut so many recipes from this book that we may just have enough for another entire book one day by just using those on the cutting room floor. I tried to select recipes for this book that would help you learn, that

Introduction

would provide basic skills, and that would provide you a road map for having an array of recipes of your very own for your family. Pull from old recipes, pull from new recipes, and put together dishes and meals that your kids will one day say were their *most favorite of all.*

That's the funny thing about a recipe: Much like an heirloom, the most meaningful ones are meaningful to you because of the people, moments, and memories you've had with them. They are cherished and intertwined in our minds—the taste of the food coupled with the experiences we have with it, or the person who made it for us. They create a feeling in your heart that lives forever. Without those connections, it's just another recipe.

GATHER TOGETHER

Another common thread you'll find in the following pages is the notion of gathering. Coming together in the kitchen, laughing and cooking, making memories. The days are busy in today's world. I can promise you that with three young kids in four sports each, two working parents, extended family and friends, church, coaching, and all that comes with life—we have just about as busy a schedule as anyone.

Making, not finding, time to sit down together around the table for a meal is of the utmost importance to us. Sure, there are days that we eat dinner at 8:00 p.m. at the ballpark concession stand after a game, but nine times out of ten, we're at home cooking a simple meal and sitting together at the table. It's the light conversations and laughter that I love the most, the highs and lows of the day that are shared. Sharing a blessing and a meal, enjoying each other's company and good food with no phones or TVs to distract our fellowship and nourishment. It doesn't have to be fancy; it just has to be a part of your routine.

The holidays are often a time when friends and family gather, take the time to cook and bake old family recipes, set a proper table, and sit down to enjoy a meal. I challenge you not to save these rituals for special occasions or holidays alone. Make this practice a part of your everyday, and I bet you'll be surprised by how fulfilling and enriching these tasks can be.

I'm not a classically trained chef; I'm a home cook who was trained by the generations before me and those who inspired me in the kitchen. Even if you are starting with zero skills in the kitchen, you too can learn and grow just by trying. Practice makes perfect, as they say, and even after years of making my favorite recipes, they get better and better each time I make them (with a few fails along the way). Don't let those treasured family recipes fall by the wayside—continue their legacy.

It is my hope that you take these challenges and capture a collection of recipes for yourself, both old and new. Take this book and get your hands dirty in the old-school techniques and skills, attempt to master a few recipes, and perhaps come away with a signature recipe of your very own. Gather together around the table to create memories that will be cherished for future generations of your family.

KITCHEN ESSENTIALS

TOOLS AND EQUIPMENT

Growing up, I spent an ample amount of time in the kitchen alongside multiple generations of my family. From this, I not only gained a knack for cooking and baking, but also took note of the tried-and-true kitchen tools that one should always have on hand. I feel lucky to have inherited many of these kitchen tools from my grandparents and other family branches. I have sourced the few pieces I was missing from my favorite antique shops. There's just something about vintage cooking and baking tools—they make cooking fun, make food better, and hold up better than today's tools. (Although I must admit to liking some modern kitchen tools. They can be very helpful at times.)

- COOKIE CUTTERS
- FOOD PROCESSOR (LARGE AND MINI CHOPPER)
- GLASS JUICER
- MEASURING CUPS
- MEASURING SPOONS
- MIXING BOWLS
- PASTRY BLENDER
- PASTRY BRUSH
- POTATO MASHER
- SILICONE BAKING MAT
- SPATULA
- TEA KETTLE
- WOODEN ROLLING PIN

POTS AND PANS

The key to executing a recipe perfectly: Have the proper pots and pans. This category of kitchen essentials can be overwhelming, as there are so many different sizes, shapes, and materials, all yielding different results. Over the years, my cabinets have grown full of a great assortment, but this is a go-to list that every kitchen should start with.

- CAST-IRON CORNBREAD PAN
- CAST-IRON SKILLET
- DUTCH OVEN
- ROASTING PAN
- SAUCEPAN
- SAUTÉ PAN
- STOCKPOT
- WOK

Introduction

16

BAKING

Learning good recipes is only half of the battle when it comes to baking—you have to make sure you have the proper equipment to help create the classics. These tried-and-true baking basics are something every kitchen needs.

- BAKING SHEETS
- CAKE AND PIE PANS
- HAND MIXER

- LOAF PAN
- MUFFIN TIN
- STAND MIXER

PANTRY

Growing up, I remember my grandmother's pantry was always stocked full of dry ingredients, allowing her to make any recipe at a moment's notice without even going to the store. Her shelves were lined with large glass jars that were labeled with the contents inside. My sister and I would play in her pantry for hours and grab handfuls of crackers, candies, and more. My mom and I picked up this habit from my grandmother, and today you can find the same essentials stocked in each of our pantries within jars. Here's a list of pantry goods to serve as a guide for stocking your own.

- BAKING POWDER AND BAKING SODA
- CHOCOLATE CHIPS
- FLOUR
- OATS
- OILS
- PASTAS

- QUINOA
- SUGAR, BROWN SUGAR, AND POWDERED SUGAR
- VANILLA EXTRACT
- WHITE AND BROWN RICE

CHINA CABINET

Peeking in someone's china cabinet can tell you a lot about them and their family. In my collection, you will find textured linens, my grandmother's china, and vintage pieces I've claimed as my own from antique shops from over the years. Your china cabinet is a story about your family that keeps being told. The more pieces you collect, entertain with, and inherit, the more rich with memories that story becomes.

Linens: Obviously, table linens are a huge component when it comes to serving and entertaining. I've taken this into consideration over the years through my tabletop brand by creating timeless base-layer linens, meant to layer with new patterns for holidays and special occasions. I love having a clean and simple table set in my home, which I add to when guests come over. A good base layer includes:

- COCKTAIL AND DINNER NAPKINS
- PLACEMATS
- TABLE RUNNER
- TABLECLOTH

Dinnerware: In my dining room hutch, you can find my grandmother's fine china, which I was lucky enough to inherit, alongside a beautiful set of dinnerware from my own wedding. This is a good place to start with larger sets, and adding over time is a great way to grow your collection while collecting things you love. A full set for eight is a great base.

- BREAD, SALAD AND DINNER PLATES
- CEREAL BOWLS
- PASTA BOWLS
- SILVERWARE

Drinkware: Depending on how often you host, your glassware collection may vary too. Regardless of your hosting style, here are a few basics I recommend for your home.

- CHAMPAGNE FLUTES
- COCKTAIL COUPES
- JUICE GLASSES
- OLD-FASHIONED OR ROCKS GLASSES
- RED AND WHITE WINEGLASSES
- WATER GLASSES

Servingware: A delicious meal is elevated tenfold when accompanied by proper serving pieces to dish it up for your family.

- BUTTER DISH
- CAKE STAND
- CARVING KNIFE
- GRAVY BOAT
- SMALL AND LARGE PLATTERS
- SOUP TUREEN

19

HEIRLOOMED KITCHEN BASICS

HOW TO FLOUR A CAKE PAN

All-purpose flour

Butter, lard, or neutral oil

As my own little kiddos start helping more and more in the kitchen, there are so many things I remember learning for the first time from my own childhood—how to flour a cake pan is one of those.

Before you begin, ensure that the cake pan is completely dry, as drips of water will inhibit a nice, cleanly coated pan.

Lightly grease the entire surface area of your cake pan. I generally use whatever grease is actually being used in the recipe, such as lard, butter, or oil, since it's already handy. Use a small piece of waxed paper or a paper towel to spread it evenly across the surface of the pan. Be sure to grease the tiny crevices of the pan as well as the bottom and sides.

Pour a small pile of flour into the center of pan, and then lightly shake and toss it around to coat the entire pan with flour. Ensure you tilt and tap the pan around so all areas, including the sides of the pan, are coated completely.

HOW TO SEPARATE AN EGG

After many years of practice, here are my best tips for separating an egg—but truth be told, the best way to master this one is just to give it some good practice.

Gather the eggs along with two bowls, one for capturing the egg whites and the other for the egg yolks.

Carefully crack the eggshell over the first bowl, trying to gently tap the egg in the very middle of the shell, slightly rotating it around to get a nice, even break.

Separate the eggshell, holding it straight up and down vertically, so the bottom half of the eggshell becomes a "bowl" to hold the egg yolk. Be careful to ensure no bits of shell fall into the bowl.

Allow the egg whites to drip into the first bowl you are working over, slightly tipping the shells and gently transferring the yolk back and forth between each half of the broken eggshell to allow as much of the egg whites as possible to fall into the bowl below. Be sure not to break the yolk in the transferring process or it will contaminate your egg whites and you'll have to start over with a new egg. Place the yolks into the second bowl.

HOW TO MAKE A ROUX

Butter

Flour

A must-master skill for any cook, but particularly Southern ones, is how to make a good roux, the essential base for any gravy, sauce, or stew. This takes practice and time but an important kitchen skill to master for any home cook.

WHAT IS A ROUX? A combination of flour and fat, which is commonly used as a thickening agent in the cooking of gravy, sauces, and stews.

In a pan, melt butter over medium heat until bubbly. Add in an amount of flour equal to your chosen portion of butter—for example, 2 tablespoons butter to 2 tablespoons flour.

Stir the flour and butter together with a fork or whisk until thickened.

For a white roux, often used to thicken sauces, that will take 2 to 5 minutes.

For a blond roux, often used in soups, cook until it smells a bit "toasty," usually 5 to 10 minutes.

A medium-brown roux takes 15 to 30 minutes, and a dark brown roux takes 30 to 45 minutes. Both medium and dark-brown roux are used in making most gumbos.

NOTES: Roux comes in many forms: white, brown, medium brown, dark brown, and variations of these. The roux I usually make is white to blond, but there are plenty of uses for darker roux.

Roux is one of those mysterious things that few people know how to make these days. Not because it's necessarily difficult, but because it isn't often taught, or even thought of, when it comes to cooking in the everyday kitchen.

HOW TO CLEAN CAST IRON

Known to impart wonderful flavor and cook anything from bacon to bread, these iron heirlooms often get a bad reputation when it comes to cleaning. However, if treated right, they will last you generations. There are many dos and don'ts when it comes to your cast iron, but I have my own simple advice for how to properly clean your skillet.

After cooking in your cast iron, let it cool. When it has cooled completely, wet it with warm water and pour a few spoonfuls kosher or sea salt on it.

Use the salt to scour the pan clean with a sponge. You can dry it with a dish towel.

At this point, I like to place the pan in a warm oven so it dries completely.

What you're really trying to avoid at all times is rust, and water left on cast iron will turn to rust. So always make sure to dry your pan thoroughly.

NOTE: If your cast iron does rust, use steel wool to scour the pan until all the rust is removed, then heat it dry in the oven or on the stovetop and apply a very light coating of oil before storing.

METRIC CONVERSION CHART

VOLUME MEASUREMENTS		WEIGHT MEASUREMENTS		TEMPERATURE CONVERSION	
U.S.	METRIC	U.S.	METRIC	FAHRENHEIT	CELSIUS
1 TEASPOON	5 ML	½ OUNCE	15 G	250	120
1 TABLESPOON	15 ML	1 OUNCE	30 G	300	150
¼ CUP	60 ML	3 OUNCES	90 G	325	160
⅓ CUP	75 ML	4 OUNCES	115 G	350	180
½ CUP	125 ML	8 OUNCES	225 G	375	190
⅔ CUP	150 ML	12 OUNCES	350 G	400	200
¾ CUP	175 ML	1 POUND	450 G	425	220
1 CUP	250 ML	2¼ POUNDS	1 KG	450	230

STANDARD KITCHEN CONVERSIONS

	DRY MEASURES		LIQUID MEASURES	
TEASPOON	TABLESPOON	CUP	FL OZ.	PINT
3	1	1/16	1/2	1/32
6	2	1/8	1	1/16
12	4	1/4	2	1/8
18	6	3/8	3	—
24	8	1/2	4	1/4
36	12	3/4	6	—
48	16	1	8	1/2
96	32	2	16	1
—	64	4	32	2
—	256	16	128	8

TINY MEASURES

DASH	1/2 TEASPOON
PINCH	1/16 TEASPOON
SMIDGEN	1/32 TEASPOON
DROP	1/72 TEASPOON

1 teaspoon dried herbs = 1 tablespoon fresh herbs

COMMON SUBSTITUTIONS

1 TEASPOON BAKING POWDER	1/4 TEASPOON BAKING SODA + 1/2 TEASPOON CREAM OF TARTAR
1 TEASPOON CREAM OF TARTAR	2 TEASPOONS VINEGAR OR LEMON JUICE
1 CUP UNSALTED BUTTER	1 CUP SHORTENING
1 CUP BUTTERMILK	1 TABLESPOON LEMON JUICE + 1 CUP MILK

MEAT TEMPERATURES

USDA GUIDELINES (BEFORE RESTING)

BEEF

RARE	130° F
MEDIUM-RARE	145° F
MEDIUM	160° F
MEDIUM-WELL	165° F
WELL	170° F
GROUND BEEF	160° F

LAMB

RARE	120° F
MEDIUM-RARE	125° F
MEDIUM	130° F
MEDIUM-WELL	145° F
WELL	150° F
GROUND LAMB	160° F

POULTRY

WHOLE BIRD	145° F (ALL)
THIGHS	
LEGS	
WINGS	
BONELESS	
GROUND	

PORK

MEDIUM	160° F
WELL	170° F
GROUND PORK	160° F

Grass Fed • Free Range • Heritage Breed

BREAKFAST
&
BRUNCH

❖—❖

Breakfast and brunch are
eternally romantic and effortless
whether sweet or savory.
The morning meal is my favorite.

Grandma's Waffles and IceMilk

SERVES 6 TO 10

2 cups all-purpose flour

2 tablespoons sugar

2 teaspoons baking powder

¼ teaspoon salt

⅔ cup unsalted butter, melted

1¾ cups milk

2 large eggs

1 teaspoon vanilla extract

Vanilla frozen yogurt

Fruit toppings, of choice
(I prefer fresh peaches and
blueberries)

WHAT IS ICEMILK?
IceMilk is a frozen treat
similar to ice cream, but
instead is made with skim
milk. IceMilk is believed to
have been created sometime
around 1840. Today's
version is frozen yogurt.

Grandma's Waffles and IceMilk is a meal that reminds me of my childhood in Florida. Growing up, my grandma would make this for dinner for us each time we came to visit—what a treat! And it inspired the original name of my company, IceMilk Aprons that went on to become Heirloomed.

Preheat the waffle iron.

In a large bowl, whisk together the flour, sugar, baking powder, and salt.

In a small bowl, whisk together the butter, milk, eggs, and vanilla.

Add the wet ingredients to the dry ingredients. Whisk until well combined, aiming to get rid of any lumps.

Pour about ¼ cup of batter into the hot waffle iron and let cook until golden, approximately 2 minutes, or until the waffle iron easily separates when you try to open it. Repeat this process until all the waffle batter is used.

To make the waffles into "IceMilk Waffles," serve with a scoop of vanilla frozen yogurt, as well as your favorite fruit toppings.

Classic Buttermilk Pancakes

MAKES 8 PANCAKES

1¼ cups all-purpose flour

¼ cup sugar

1 teaspoon baking powder

1 teaspoon baking soda

Pinch of kosher salt

¼ cup buttermilk

1 large egg

¼ cup vegetable oil

Butter, for greasing

Topping of choice: blueberries, butter, whipped cream, syrup, or a dusting of powdered sugar

Homemade pancakes served with a pat of butter and drizzled with warm maple syrup are about as traditional a staple for a weekend family breakfast as one can find. They are even more delicious when made with a splash of homemade buttermilk for that extra tang. My kids love to help make pancakes on the griddle, and especially love when Grandma skillfully makes them in the fancy shapes of various animals and letters.

Preheat the griddle or a skillet over medium heat.

In a medium bowl, mix the flour, sugar, baking powder, baking soda, salt, buttermilk, egg, and oil until combined. Do not overmix.

Grease the griddle with a few pats of butter. Pour ¼ cup of batter onto the griddle for each pancake. Cook for about 1 minute or until the batter starts to set around edges and little bubbles or pockets begin to appear on the side of the pancake.

Flip and cook for about 1 minute more or until you see the pancakes are browned on the other side and cooked through. Repeat with remaining batter.

Serve with toppings of choice.

Thick-Cut French Toast

SERVES 6

Butter, for greasing and serving

2 large eggs

Zest of 1 orange

1 tablespoon ground cinnamon

¼ cup heavy cream

10 to 12 slices thick-cut bread

Powdered sugar, syrup, berries, whipped cream, for serving

French toast is my personal choice when it comes to a weekend breakfast. There is just something so comforting about waking up on a lazy weekend morning to make this with the kids.

Preheat the griddle or skillet over medium heat. Toss in a few pats of butter to coat the pan.

In a large bowl, mix the eggs, orange zest, cinnamon, and heavy cream together.

Dip slices of bread in the mixture, making sure both sides are coated.

Place the bread slices on the griddle and cook on each side for 2 to 3 minutes or until golden brown. You will need to cook in batches.

Top the French toast with powdered sugar, butter, syrup, berries, or whipped cream to serve.

Brie, Sausage, and Sage Casserole

SERVES 8 TO 12

1 (8-ounce) round of Brie

1 pound ground hot pork sausage

6 slices white bread of choice

1 cup grated Parmesan cheese

7 large eggs

3 cups heavy cream, divided

2 cups fat-free milk

1 teaspoon dried rubbed sage

1 teaspoon seasoned salt

1 teaspoon dry mustard

Chopped green onions (optional), for garnishing

This recipe comes straight from Aunt Jo, and it's the perfect make-ahead breakfast casserole for holiday mornings, brunches, and when family comes to town. It's creamy and filling, and full of savory flavors.

Lightly grease a 9 x 13-inch baking dish.

Trim and discard the rind from the Brie. Cut the cheese into 1-inch cubes and set aside.

In a large skillet over medium heat, cook the sausage until crumbled and no longer pink, 8 to 10 minutes. Drain the grease from the sausage.

Cut the crusts from the bread and place them evenly in the baking dish. Layer the bread slices on top and then add the cooked sausage, Brie, and Parmesan cheese.

In a large bowl, whisk together 5 eggs, 2 cups heavy cream, and the milk, sage, seasoned salt, and mustard. Pour evenly over cheeses. Cover and chill for 8 hours.

When ready to bake, preheat the oven to 350 degrees F.

In a medium bowl, whisk together the remaining 2 eggs and the remaining 1 cup heavy cream. Pour evenly over chilled mixture. Bake casserole for 50 minutes or until set, and garnish with green onions to serve if using.

Flaky Buttermilk Biscuits

MAKES 6 LARGE BISCUITS

2 cups all-purpose flour, plus more for flouring

1/4 teaspoon baking soda

1 tablespoon baking powder

1 1/4 teaspoons kosher salt

6 tablespoons cold lard

1 cup cold buttermilk

This made-from-scratch biscuit recipe is my go-to family recipe from my stepmom's family in rural Kentucky. It yields tender and flaky Southern biscuits. For many, making biscuits doesn't come from a recipe, but instead from years of making them alongside someone in the kitchen and trying to master the same consistency time after time.

Preheat the oven to 375 degrees F.

In a large bowl, combine the flour, baking soda, baking powder, and salt and mix well. Using a fork or pastry blender, cut the cold lard into the flour mixture until it resembles a coarse, pebble-like mixture.

Pour the buttermilk into the mixture and stir just a few turns until combined. Don't overmix as it will make the biscuits tough.

Generously flour the countertop or cutting board, as well as your hands. The dough will be rather wet and sticky at this point. Pat the dough out until it is approximately 1/2 inch thick and then add another dusting of flour across the top of the dough.

Proceed to fold the dough over onto itself a few times, finally patting it to about 1 inch thick. Remember not to overwork the dough or ever use a rolling pin, because it will make for tough biscuits.

(continued)

NOTE: The true secret to mastering this family recipe is using very cold ingredients and not working the dough too much with your hands. For the softest and flakiest biscuits, White Lily is always our choice of flour.

36

(continued)

Use a biscuit cutter to cut out the biscuits. Do not twist and turn, but instead cleanly punch out each biscuit. This will prevent "sealing" the edges of the dough. You can dip the biscuit cutter in a little flour before each punch to ensure that no dough sticks.

Once you cut out all the biscuits, take the leftover dough scraps and gently pat them to about 1 inch thick. This will allow you to cut a final biscuit or two.

Choose a small, high-sided pan (I generally use my 8-inch cake pan) and place biscuits next to each other so they are touching. Place the pan in the oven and then immediately turn up the heat to 450 degrees. This will give the biscuits a little crispness on the outside while keeping them moist on the inside.

Bake for approximately 10 minutes, or until lightly browned. Try to refrain from opening the oven door to peek inside—this will keep the steam inside the oven, which will produce a very moist and delicious biscuit.

Classic Southern White Gravy

MAKES 2 1/2 CUPS

4 tablespoons butter

4 tablespoons flour

2 teaspoons freshly ground black pepper

1 teaspoon salt

1/2 teaspoon garlic salt

2 1/2 cups milk

Enjoy this classic white gravy, creamy and full of black pepper. The perfect topping for your breakfast or brunch Flaky Buttermilk Biscuits (page 34).

In a medium saucepan over medium heat, melt the butter and then whisk in the flour and pepper. While continuously whisking, add the salt and garlic salt.

Slowly pour in the milk and reduce the heat to low, whisking the mixture occasionally. It will thicken in about 5 minutes. Remove from the heat and serve.

Fried-Chicken Biscuits

SERVES 6

2 ⅔ cups peanut oil, for frying

FOR THE BREADING

1 cup flour

1 cup cornstarch

1 tablespoon garlic salt

2 teaspoons freshly ground black pepper

1 teaspoon paprika

1 teaspoon onion powder

1 teaspoon baking powder

½ teaspoon cayenne pepper

FOR THE BATTER

1 cup cornstarch

1 teaspoon salt

¾ cup water

2 large eggs

FOR THE CHICKEN AND BISCUITS

½ pound (6 pieces) chicken tenders

Flaky Buttermilk Biscuits (page 34)

I'd argue that the perfect breakfast is a light and fluffy biscuit with a mouthwateringly crisp and tender piece of Southern-fried chicken in the middle.

Preheat the peanut oil in a Dutch oven to 350 degrees F.

To make the breading, in a medium bowl, whisk together the flour, cornstarch, garlic salt, black pepper, paprika, onion powder, baking powder, and cayenne pepper.

To make the batter, in a second medium bowl, whisk together the cornstarch and salt, and then stir in the water and eggs to thoroughly combine.

To prepare the chicken, dip each tender into the breading, then into the batter, and then into the breading again. Shake off the excess flour and fry the chicken in small batches for about 6 minutes, turning the tenders over halfway through cooking time, until golden brown.

To serve, slice the Flaky Buttermilk Biscuits in half, place a chicken tender on one half, and top with the other half.

 NOTE: When entertaining, add a dollop of mayonnaise and a skewer with a tiny pickle to each Fried-Chicken Biscuit. Arrange them on a serving tray for a dressed-up presentation your guests will love.

Old-Fashioned Crunchy Maple Granola

MAKES ABOUT 5 CUPS

4 cups old-fashioned rolled oats (not quick-cooking)

1 cup sliced almonds

½ cup shredded coconut (preferably unsweetened)

¼ cup raw pumpkin or sunflower seeds

⅓ cup toasted wheat germ

½ cup pure maple syrup

2 tablespoons canola oil

½ teaspoon kosher salt

1 cup dried fruit, of choice (cranberries, cherries, raisins, currants)

While yummy by itself, this classic recipe for granola is also a great topping for yogurt, cereal, or other quick snacks. I love to store it in a large, vintage glass jar in the pantry and keep it on hand for busy mornings. It also makes the perfect gift to bring along with fresh yogurt and berries when friends invite you to the lake for the weekend.

Preheat the oven to 350 degrees F.

In a large bowl, toss the oats, almonds, coconut, pumpkin seeds, wheat germ, maple syrup, oil, and salt together and thoroughly combine. Spread the mixture in a single layer on a rimmed baking sheet.

Bake, tossing once during the cooking time, until golden and crisp, 25 to 30 minutes.

Add the dried fruit and stir to combine. Let cool. Store in airtight container for up to two weeks.

NOTE: My favorite thing about homemade granola is that you can easily adjust it to match what you're craving, or to your specific dietary needs. Add in more dried fruit or your favorite seeds to spruce up this recipe to your liking. I prefer dried cherries, but if not eating the granola right away, I keep the cherries separate and mix them in right before use to keep their moist consistency.

Crispy Bacon, Two Ways

SERVES 8

1 pound bacon, of choice

Here are two ways to make the most delicious, crispy bacon for breakfast, lunch, dinner, or any snack in between.

SKILLET

The classic way to cook bacon is in a skillet. You will always get a consistently crispy bacon, and plenty of grease to use for your gravy afterward. Cooking bacon this way is pretty easy. Just line the bacon in a single layer in the skillet and cook over medium heat. After a few minutes, you will start to hear that glorious crackling and sizzling sound that is the wonder of fatty bacon grease. Flip bacon to cook on the other side for a few minutes, and you're done. Some folks like it crispier, others like it less cooked, so cook to desired preference.

BAKING SHEET

The second way to cook bacon is my new personal favorite. It is even easier than a skillet, and causes less of a mess. Preheat the oven to 350 degrees F. Line a baking sheet with aluminum foil (or use a wire rack), lay strips of bacon out into a neat little row, and bake for about 20 minutes. This method is hands-off and gives you time to tend to what else is cooking on the stove. It also means you don't have to worry about grease splattering all over the kitchen. And, it provides a nice, evenly cooked bacon strip. No matter how you prefer your bacon, I think we can all agree it is one of the tastiest things you can make.

Leek and Swiss Cheese Quiche

SERVES 8

5 large eggs

1 cup heavy cream

¼ teaspoon kosher salt

1 teaspoon freshly ground
black pepper

Nana's Pie Crust (page 164)

1 to 2 leeks, sliced into medium
rings

4 green onions, chopped

1 cup shredded Swiss cheese

5 thyme sprigs, for garnishing

They say that "real men don't eat quiche," but here in the South, we beg to differ. Quiche is such a simple, make-ahead dish that can be created using a wide variety of flavor and ingredient profiles—but one that is still impressive enough to serve for parties or brunch.

Preheat the oven to 375 degrees F.

In a large bowl, beat the eggs with whisk until well blended. Add the cream, salt, and pepper.

Place the pie crust in an 8-inch quiche pan or 8-inch pie plate. Layer in half of the sliced leeks and half of the chopped green onions, and then layer half of the Swiss cheese. Repeat the layers.

Pour the egg-and-cream mixture over the leek, onion, and cheese layers. Garnish with sprigs of thyme.

Bake for 35 minutes, until quiche is firm and the top is golden. Let the quiche rest for a few minutes before slicing and serving while warm.

APPETIZERS

·:———:·

We love entertaining,
and having a good arsenal of
appetizers is the perfect
way to ensure your guests are
satisfied and comfortable in your
home. I also love having a
"go-to array of easy recipes
that I can toss together quickly
if we're invited over to
a gathering. These are a
few of my favorites.

Roadside Hot-Boiled Peanuts

MAKES 2 TO 3 POUNDS

2 to 3 pounds green (raw) peanuts in shell

8 cups water

¼ to ½ cup salt, to taste

Our family loves a good road trip and nothing brings me greater joy than seeing a hand-painted sign and stopping at a country road four-way stop to get a big, brown bag of boiled peanuts from an older gentleman dressed in overalls with a bandana tucked inside. This Southern delicacy is one everyone must try. I bring you this recipe and the good news that you can actually make up a batch for yourself.

Rinse the peanuts in colander under cold water to remove any dirt or debris.

Place the peanuts in a 5-quart slow cooker. Cover with the water, add the salt, and stir.

Cook on low heat, covered, for 24 hours or high heat for 12 hours, adding more water as needed to keep the peanuts covered. Stir occasionally, as the peanuts might float to the top, especially when they are still green. Taste and add more salt as desired.

Allow peanuts to sit in the warm-water brine for an additional 12 hours or overnight.

Serve warm or refrigerate, drained, for up to 1 week after cooking.

Southern-Style Deviled Eggs

MAKES 12 DEVILED EGGS

6 large eggs

4 tablespoons mayonnaise, of choice

2 tablespoons pickle relish

1 tablespoon apple-cider vinegar

2 teaspoons dry mustard

½ teaspoon kosher salt

Freshly ground black pepper

1 bunch green onions, green parts only, chopped

I always seem to get put in charge of making these deviled eggs for family gatherings, and I don't mind one bit! This is a Southern staple I feel I have perfected.

Hard-boil eggs for approximately 12 minutes. Allow them to cool completely in an ice-water bath. Peel, wash, and pat dry, and then slice each egg vertically.

In a medium glass bowl, spoon out the yolk from each egg. Set aside the egg whites on a plate.

Add the mayonnaise, pickle relish, vinegar, and mustard to the egg yolks. Mash and mix with a fork until the desired texture is achieved. Carefully spoon the filling back into each egg white. Sprinkle with salt and pepper. Top with green onions.

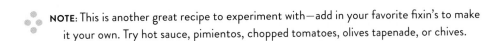

NOTE: This is another great recipe to experiment with—add in your favorite fixin's to make it your own. Try hot sauce, pimientos, chopped tomatoes, olives tapenade, or chives.

Fried Green Tomatoes

SERVES 4 TO 6

4 medium green tomatoes

2 large eggs

½ cup buttermilk

1 cup all-purpose flour

½ cup cornmeal

2 teaspoons kosher salt

½ teaspoon freshly ground black pepper

½ teaspoon cayenne pepper

½ cup plain bread crumbs

1 quart vegetable oil

Kosher salt for serving

Sour cream for serving, optional

Goat cheese and thyme for serving, optional

A COMMON QUESTION is if a "green tomato" is a special variety or just a tomato that hasn't fully ripened. The answer is the latter, simple as that.

A must-try Southern classic for your kitchen during the summer. Enjoy with your favorite sauce as an appetizer or atop a sandwich for lunch.

Slice the tomatoes to a medium thickness and place on a paper towel–lined baking sheet to absorb some of the moisture. Set aside. Have a second paper towel–lined baking sheet ready.

In a small bowl, whisk the eggs. Add the buttermilk, stirring to combine.

In a medium bowl, combine the flour, cornmeal, salt, black pepper, and cayenne pepper.

Pour the bread crumbs onto a plate and set aside.

In a large cast-iron skillet over medium heat, heat the oil until tiny bubbles form around the end of a wooden spoon dipped into the oil. Dip the tomatoes, one slice at a time, in the flour mixture, then the egg mixture, and then the flour mixture again. Finally, fully coat the dipped tomatoes in bread crumbs. Using tongs, carefully place the tomatoes into the hot oil.

Cook tomato slices on one side for approximately 2 minutes, turning to check for golden color. Flip and cook on the other side for approximately 2 more minutes. Remove from the skillet and place on the prepared baking sheet. Immediately sprinkle salt on top for perfect seasoning.

Serve warm, plain, or with dollop of sour cream or sprinkling of goat cheese and thyme.

NOTE: Anyone who has ever grown tomatoes in their own garden knows that when the plants begin to overproduce, there are only so many tomato recipe variations you can make at one time. So, utilizing the green ones before they've ripened is useful as well as delicious.

51

Savory Spiced Nuts

MAKES 6 CUPS

3 cups unsalted, whole cashews

3 cups shelled pecan halves

2 tablespoons fresh rosemary leaves, chopped

1 to 2 teaspoons cayenne pepper

Juice of ½ orange

1 tablespoon dark brown sugar

1 tablespoon pure maple syrup

1 tablespoon butter, melted

Kosher salt, to taste

This is a salty, sweet, spiced snack for setting out during holiday seasons, or year-round as the perfect nibble.

Preheat the oven to 375 degrees F. Grease a rimmed baking sheet.

Place the nuts on a baking sheet and let warm in the oven for 10 minutes. While the nuts are warming, in a large bowl, mix together the rosemary, cayenne, orange juice, brown sugar, maple syrup, and butter. Toss the warmed nuts in the rosemary mixture until fully coated. Season with salt. Return to the oven and bake for an additional 10 minutes, stirring often. Serve warm.

IF YOU HAVE EVER VISITED my home, then you know I always have a bowl of pistachios on the kitchen island to snack on. During the holiday season, I don't waste any time jumping on the opportunity to spice things up—literally—with this recipe.

NOTE: Typically, I'd want to put parchment on the baking sheet for easier cleanup, but when roasting the nuts, it works best to put them directly on the pan. This will ensure that they turn out nice and crispy—just make sure to grease the pan well.

White Cheddar and Herbed Pimiento Cheese

SERVES 12

1½ cups sour cream

½ cup Homemade Mayo (page 205) or mayonnaise of choice

1 (4-ounce) can pimientos, with liquid, optional

1 teaspoon Worcestershire sauce

½ teaspoon coarse kosher salt

½ teaspoon freshly ground black pepper

1 bunch fresh herbs (flat-leaf parsley, cilantro, chives)

2 to 3 green onions, thinly sliced

8 ounces cream cheese, room temperature

1 pound freshly grated white cheddar cheese

Homemade pimiento cheese is one of those staples that I always have on hand. This revered recipe is delicious at any time of year, but is especially welcomed in the South during Masters week. I love the spin on this recipe, which fills it with fresh herbs and white cheddar, giving it a beautiful look on the table.

In a medium bowl, mix together the sour cream, mayonnaise, and pimientos with their liquid (if using) until combined. Add the Worcestershire sauce, salt, and pepper.

Chop the herbs. Fold the herbs and green onions into the sour cream mixture.

Stir in the softened cream cheese and then fold in the white cheddar cheese until just blended.

Refrigerate until serving.

—❖ **HIGHLIGHTS** ❖—

Make this recipe into an easy, thoughtful food gift. Pop some White Cheddar and Herbed Pimiento Cheese into a Mason jar, pair it with a pack of crackers, add a tea towel, and gift it to your spring hostess or neighbors.

SALADS
&
SOUPS

·:—·:

Salads and soups are
classic starters, or perfect
for a light lunch. Seasonal
ingredients and special
occasions make these
some of my favorites.

Tangy Dijon Salad Dressing

MAKES ABOUT ¾ CUP

¼ cup apple-cider vinegar

½ cup extra-virgin olive oil

2 teaspoons Dijon mustard

1 tablespoon minced garlic

1 teaspoon sea salt, plus more if needed

½ teaspoon freshly ground black pepper, plus more if needed

Having a few go-to homemade salad dressings in your arsenal is a must. In this recipe, the acidity and tang from the vinegar and Dijon goes perfectly with a freshly chopped salad of your choosing, such as Apple Harvest Salad (below).

In a blender, blend the vinegar, oil, mustard, garlic, salt, and pepper until completely combined. Or, combine all ingredients in a Mason jar and shake well. Taste for salt and pepper and add more if needed.

Apple Harvest Salad

SERVES 6 TO 8

1 (5-ounce) bag of mixed greens

1½ cups cooked farro

2 large seasonal apples, of choice, diced

½ cup toasted pumpkin seeds

½ cup halved pecans

½ cup blue cheese crumbles

Tangy Dijon Salad Dressing (above)

I love this Apple Harvest Salad. It's the perfect way to layer in all the flavors of fall and to make sure that I keep salad in our family's routine.

In a large bowl, combine the mixed greens, farro, apples, pumpkin seeds, pecans, and blue cheese. Toss with the dressing when ready to serve.

Tarragon Chicken Salad

SERVES 10 TO 12

4 boneless, skinless chicken breasts

¼ cup slivered almonds

¼ cup Homemade Mayo (page 205) or mayonnaise of choice

2 tablespoons sour cream

Juice of 1 lemon

1 bunch fresh tarragon leaves

Kosher salt, to taste

Freshly ground black pepper, to taste

There are two kinds of people out there—those who love sweet chicken salad and those who love savory. If you're team savory, like me, then you will love this Tarragon Chicken Salad.

Fill a large pot with salted water and bring to a boil. Add the chicken breasts and cook for 15 to 20 minutes, until chicken is fully cooked and no longer pink. Remove and pat dry with paper towels. Completely cool in the refrigerator. Once cool, cut the chicken into ½-inch chunks, place in a large bowl, and set aside.

In a small, dry skillet, toast the slivered almonds over medium heat, tossing constantly for approximately 1 minute, or just long enough to give them a slightly brown color. Transfer to a small bowl to cool.

In another small bowl, combine the mayonnaise and sour cream. Stir in the lemon juice and tarragon.

Add the mayonnaise mixture to the cubed chicken, slowly folding it into the chicken to get the preferred consistency. Once the texture is to your liking, add the toasted almonds and salt and pepper.

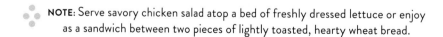 **NOTE:** Serve savory chicken salad atop a bed of freshly dressed lettuce or enjoy as a sandwich between two pieces of lightly toasted, hearty wheat bread.

Picnic Potato Salad

SERVES 12

3 pounds Honey Gold potatoes, unpeeled

3 or 4 large eggs, for garnishing

1 bunch green onions, roughly chopped

1 bunch fresh dill, roughly chopped

1 bunch flat-leaf Italian parsley, roughly chopped

Kosher salt, to taste

Freshly ground black pepper, to taste

FOR THE VINAIGRETTE

3 tablespoons apple-cider vinegar

4 teaspoons whole grain mustard

1 teaspoon mustard seeds

1/2 cup extra-virgin olive oil

Our twist on the classic potato salad recipe makes for a great side dish when entertaining guests. I prefer this light, vinegar-based version to those with a heavy mayonnaise base.

To make the potato salad, in a large pot of salted water, boil the potatoes until tender. Drain and set aside to cool.

In a small saucepan, boil the eggs until soft boiled. Drain and set aside in ice water bath to cool.

To make the vinaigrette, in a large bowl, whisk together the vinegar, mustard, and mustard seeds. Gradually add in the olive oil until emulsified.

Halve the potatoes and add to the vinaigrette and toss to coat. Add the green onions, dill, and parsley and toss to combine. Season with salt and pepper.

Halve or roughly chop the soft-boiled eggs and use for garnish to serve.

Tomato Bisque

SERVES 6 TO 8

¼ cup salted butter

1 medium white onion, diced

2 tablespoons balsamic vinegar

2 garlic cloves, minced

4 tablespoons tomato paste

2 (28-ounce) cans whole tomatoes

7 cups vegetable or chicken stock

½ cup heavy cream

1 teaspoon salt

½ teaspoon freshly ground black pepper

Fresh herb sprigs, like basil or thyme, for garnishing

Paired with a creamy, warm Sourdough and Fontina Grilled Cheese Sandwich (page 79), this bisque recipe is unmatched.

In a large stock pot over medium heat, melt the butter. Add the onion, vinegar, and garlic and sauté until the onion is softened.

Stir in the tomato paste and cook for 5 minutes.

Add the tomatoes with their juices and stock, and increase heat to high to bring mixture to a boil. Reduce to a simmer and cover. Let cook for 50 minutes, stirring often, and then remove from the heat.

Using an immersion blender, blend mixture until smooth. Add the heavy cream, salt, and pepper and blend until well incorporated.

If needed, reheat soup over medium until desired temperature is reached. Garnish with herb sprigs and serve.

Butternut Squash Bisque

1 tablespoon unsalted butter

1 tablespoon canola oil

½ cup diced onion

¾ cup diced carrots

4 cups peeled and cubed butternut squash

3 cups vegetable stock

Salt, to taste

Freshly ground black pepper, to taste

Ground nutmeg, to taste

½ cup heavy cream, optional

I know I am in the minority with this, but I can eat soup year-round, no matter the temperature outside. There is just something so classic and comforting about this hearty Butternut Squash Bisque. It's one of my favorites during the fall with its full flavors.

In a large pot over medium heat, melt the butter and heat the oil together until hot. Stir in the onion and cook until tender.

Add the carrots and squash. Pour in the vegetable stock and season with salt, pepper, and nutmeg. Bring to a boil, reduce heat, and simmer until vegetables are tender, 8 to 10 minutes.

In a blender or food processor, purée the soup mixture until smooth. You may need to blend the soup in batches. Return to the pot and stir in the cream, if using. Place the pot back on stove and heat through, but do not boil. Serve warm with a dash of nutmeg.

 NOTE: Crème fraîche, pumpkin seeds, and thyme make great garnishes for this soup as well.

Feel Better Chicken Noodle Soup

SERVES 6 TO 8

2 tablespoons extra-virgin olive oil

4 carrots, sliced

4 celery stalks, sliced

1 yellow onion, diced

3 garlic cloves

2 tablespoons fresh thyme

1 teaspoon salt, plus more to taste

½ teaspoon freshly ground black pepper, plus more to taste

10 cups chicken stock or broth

1 (12-ounce) bag wide egg noodles

2 cups shredded chicken

Juice of ½ lemon

2 tablespoons minced fresh parsley or a sprig of fresh thyme, for garnishing

Homemade soup can do no wrong, in my opinion. This classic recipe is one I like to make when the weather cools down or the sniffles show up around our house. The kids love a good, brothy soup, and this family favorite is their most requested soup of all.

In a large pot over medium-high heat, combine the oil, carrots, celery, and onion. Sauté about 5 minutes, until vegetables are tender, and then add the garlic, thyme, salt, and pepper, and sauté for another minute.

Add the chicken stock and noodles, and bring to a boil over high heat. Reduce the heat to a simmer to let the noodles cook until tender, about 10 minutes.

Add the chicken and lemon juice right before serving; simmer until chicken is heated throughout. Add more salt and pepper, if desired. Garnish with parsley.

Everyone's Favorite Turkey Chili

SERVES 12

2 pounds ground turkey

1 tablespoon extra-virgin olive oil

2 cups chopped white onions

2 tablespoons chopped garlic

1 tablespoon dried oregano

2 bay leaves

3 tablespoons chili powder

2 teaspoons ground cumin

1 cup canned, diced tomatoes, drained

2 (29-ounce) cans tomato sauce

1 teaspoon salt, plus more to taste

1/2 teaspoon freshly ground black pepper, plus more to taste

2 (15-ounce) cans red kidney beans, drained and rinsed

1 (15-ounce) can chili beans, drained

Shredded cheddar cheese, for garnishing

Sour cream, for garnishing

1 jalapeño, thinly sliced, for garnishing

I make this recipe almost weekly for my family in the cooler months. It is simple, filling, and a fan favorite among all my family members—which I always consider a big win. We prefer the lighter version with ground turkey, but are also known to substitute deer meat when we have our freezer stocked.

In a large stockpot over medium heat, brown the ground turkey until fully cooked.

Once browned, add the oil, onions, garlic, oregano, bay leaves, chili powder, and cumin. Stir well and cook for 5 minutes.

Add the tomatoes, tomato sauce, salt, and pepper. Bring the mixture to a boil, reduce the heat to a simmer, and let cook for 15 minutes, stirring occasionally.

Add the kidney and chili beans and cook, stirring occasionally, for about 10 minutes.

Serve the chili with cheddar cheese, sour cream, and a few sliced jalapeños for heat.

 NOTE: Other garnishes we enjoy with this chili are bacon crumbles, avocado, and hot sauce. We always have a side of cornbread or Fritos corn chips for dipping, which add the perfect crunch.

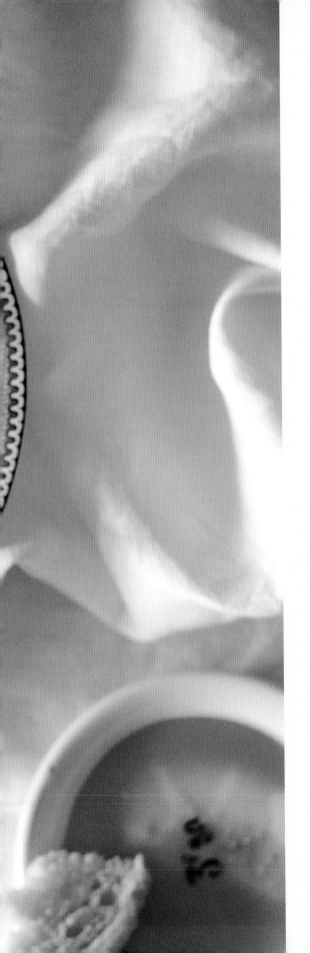

MAIN DISHES

—◆—

There is nothing quite
like gathering around the table
for a home-cooked meal.
It doesn't have to be hard or fussy,
yet it's magical all the same.

Homemade Chicken Pot Pie

SERVES 8

FOR THE PIE CRUST

1½ cups flour, plus more for flouring

Dash of salt

¾ cup shortening

5 tablespoons cold water

FOR THE FILLING

6 tablespoons unsalted butter

1 yellow onion, finely chopped

3 large celery stalks, diced

3 large carrots, peeled and diced

1 russet potato, peeled and diced

1 teaspoon kosher salt, plus more for sprinkling

½ teaspoon freshly ground black pepper

1 teaspoon chopped fresh thyme

¼ teaspoon celery seed

2 cups cooked, chopped chicken breasts

1 cup fresh or frozen peas

½ cup all-purpose flour

3 cups chicken stock

¼ cup milk

1 large egg

This classic entrée makes a family dinner that is loved by parent and child alike. Between the creamy, hearty filling and the crispy, buttery crust, this pot-pie recipe is one to write home about. It makes a comforting meal-train drop-off family dinner too.

Preheat the oven to 400 degrees F.

To make the pie crust, in a medium bowl, mix together the flour, salt, and shortening with 2 forks or a pastry blender until it forms a coarse, pebble-like texture. Stir in the water until a dough forms and turn out onto waxed paper. Shape into a ball and place in refrigerator for 15 minutes to chill.

While the dough is chilling, make the filling. In a large pot over medium heat, melt the butter and sauté the onion, celery, carrots, and potato. Add the salt, pepper, thyme, and celery seed. Cook, stirring occasionally, until the onion is translucent and veggies are tender.

Add the chicken, peas, and flour and stir continuously for 3 more minutes.

Stir in the chicken stock and bring the mixture to a boil. Stir often and cook at a low boil until thickened, about 5 minutes. Stir in the milk, and then turn off the heat and let mixture rest for 10 minutes.

To assemble the pot pie, divide the pie-crust dough ball into two even halves and place on a floured board or countertop. Roll out both halves to fit a 9-inch pie pan.

Fit the bottom pie crust into the pie pan. Scoop the chicken filling into the pie crust. Fit the top pie crust over the filling, and press together the edges to create a seal.

In a small bowl, whisk the egg. Brush the egg wash on top of pie crust to give a golden, crisp finish. Sprinkle with kosher salt, if desired. Cut a few vents in the top of the crust to allow steam to escape during baking.

Place the pot pie on a baking sheet and bake for 45 to 60 minutes, or until golden brown. If the edges of pot pie become too brown before it is finished baking, cover with aluminum foil. Cool the pot pie for 20 minutes before serving.

Thick-Cut BLT Club

SERVES 4

1 pound thick-cut bacon, of choice

3 large beefsteak or heirloom tomatoes

Salt, to taste

Freshly ground black pepper, to taste

8 slices white bread, of choice

⅓ cup Homemade Mayo (page 205) or mayonnaise of choice

1 (5-ounce) bag arugula

This classic BLT recipe is one you simply must have in your repertoire. Highlight the perfect summer tomato with this simple, delicious sandwich.

Preheat the oven to 375 degrees F.

Place the bacon strips in a single layer on a baking sheet lined with aluminum foil. Bake until just crisp, 8 to 10 minutes. When the bacon is done, transfer to a paper towel–lined plate to drain.

Slice the tomatoes, and then sprinkle with salt and pepper. Transfer to a paper towel to absorb some of the liquid.

Toast the slices of bread and set aside until ready to assemble the sandwiches.

To assemble, spread a thick layer of mayonnaise on each slice of bread. On 4 slices of bread, layer the tomatoes, bacon, and arugula. Top each with a remaining slice of bread. Slice the sandwich in half or in triangles and serve.

NOTES: Want to know the best way to get that crispy bacon perfected? Check out my tips on page 41. To really elevate this BLT recipe, swap in Fried Green Tomatoes (page 50) for extra character.

Chicken and Dumplings

SERVES 8

8 cups chicken stock

1 white or yellow onion, diced

3 large carrots, peeled and diced

3 celery stalks, diced

2 or 3 whole chicken breasts

Salt, to taste

Freshly ground black pepper, to taste

Parsley, for garnishing

2 cups Bisquick baking mix

2/3 cups whole milk

I feel so much nostalgia when I smell—or even think about— Chicken and Dumplings. My kids adore this recipe just as much as I did growing up. But I must admit, my mom still makes it better than me, every time.

In a Dutch oven over high heat, bring the stock to a boil and then add the onion, carrots, and celery.

Add the chicken breasts, cover, reduce the heat, and boil gently until the chicken is fully cooked, 12 to 15 minutes. Transfer the chicken to a cutting board. When cool enough to handle, cut the chicken into cubes, then return to the pot with the vegetables. Bring to a soft, rolling boil.

In a medium bowl, combine the Bisquick and milk to form a soft dough. Take small dollops of dough and drop into the boiling mixture until all of the dough has been used. Reduce heat to low, cover, and simmer for approximately 8 minutes, or until the dumplings are fully cooked in the center. The dumplings should be fluffy and the broth should be creamy.

Deviled Egg Salad Sandwich with Radishes

SERVES 4

6 hard-boiled eggs, peeled and patted dry

2 tablespoons Homemade Mayo (page 205) or mayonnaise of choice

1 tablespoon sweet pickle relish

¼ teaspoon dry mustard

¼ teaspoon apple-cider vinegar

Kosher salt and freshly ground black pepper, to taste

8 slices whole wheat bread

4 radishes, thinly sliced

1 bundle flat-leaf Italian parsley or watercress, roughly chopped

I much prefer a chunky-style egg salad over the mushy store-bought versions that have far too much mayo. This recipe brings in the flavors of Southern-Style Deviled Eggs (page 49) while staying true to its egg-salad roots.

Roughly chop the hard-boiled eggs to a chunky consistency, still bite-size but large enough chunks to ensure the egg salad doesn't turn into a mushy blob.

In a large bowl, combine the mayonnaise, pickle relish, dry mustard, vinegar, salt, and pepper. Stir to combine; gently fold in the chopped eggs.

Divide the egg salad mixture among 4 slices of bread. Add radish slices and parsley or watercress then top with the remaining 4 bread slices.

Sourdough and Fontina Grilled Cheese Sandwich

MAKES 1 SANDWICH

1 tablespoon butter, softened

2 slices fresh sourdough bread

¼ cup thinly sliced fontina cheese

Thyme sprig, for garnishing

NOTE: Try out different kinds of breads and cheese for an elevated play on the classic grilled cheese.

Not enough can be said about a classic grilled cheese sandwich. Served alongside a hot bowl of Tomato Bisque (page 63), this one is arguably sheer perfection.

Spread butter on one side of each slice of bread. In a small cast-iron skillet, over low-to-medium heat, place one slice of bread, buttered-side down, onto the pan. Top with fontina cheese, then place the other slice of bread on the cheese, buttered-side up.

Let the cheese melt and bread crisp to a golden brown, flipping after 3 to 5 minutes to brown the other side for an additional 3 to 5 minutes. Garnish with a sprig of thyme before serving.

Shane's Grilled BBQ Chicken

SERVES 4 TO 6

4 boneless, skinless chicken breasts

1 bottle Italian dressing, of choice

Salt, to taste

Freshly ground black pepper, to taste

BBQ Sauce (page 205)

Anything grilled is such a treat, especially in the summertime. We love to grill chicken on Sunday and make extra to have on hand for the week ahead. This tangy grilled BBQ chicken is my husband Shane's specialty, and it is our family favorite. We love the smoked flavor of grilling this recipe up on our Big Green Egg grill.

Prepare and heat grill to approximately 450 degrees F.

Place the chicken breasts in a large ziplock plastic bag and add all of the in Italian dressing, gently shaking to coat. Marinate the chicken for approximately 1 hour in the refrigerator prior to grilling.

To cook, place the chicken breasts on the hot grill and season with salt and pepper. Cover the grill and cook for 4 to 5 minutes on each side.

Brush BBQ sauce onto the chicken, grilling an additional 1 to 2 minutes per side, until the chicken is fully cooked with an internal temperature of 165 degrees F.

Remove from the grill and serve.

Baked Salmon with Sriracha Soy Sauce

SERVES 4

½ teaspoon salt, plus more to taste

¼ teaspoon freshly ground black pepper, plus more to taste

Juice of 1 large lemon

3 tablespoons low-sodium soy sauce

1 teaspoon sesame oil

1 tablespoon sriracha

4 (6-ounce) salmon fillets

I could eat fish every single day of the week. This is one of my favorite salmon recipes for its taste and simplicity. I'm typically not a big fan of spicy dishes, but this one provides just the right amount of heat to balance the salty soy sauce and sesame flavor.

Preheat the oven to 375 degrees F. Line a rimmed baking sheet with aluminum foil.

In a small mixing bowl, combine the salt, pepper, lemon juice, soy sauce, sesame oil, and sriracha. Mix until well combined.

Place the salmon on the prepared baking sheet and pour the mixture over top, reserving 2 tablespoons. Bake in for 12 minutes, or until the fish reaches internal temp of 145 degrees F. Before serving, drizzle the remaining sauce over the salmon for a beautiful, flavorful presentation.

 NOTE: For a complete meal, serve with Sesame Fried Rice (page 115).

Blackened Fish Tacos

MAKES 8 TO 10 TACOS

1 tablespoon paprika

1 tablespoon chili powder

1 tablespoon cayenne pepper

½ teaspoon kosher salt

4 to 6 tilapia or mahi-mahi fillets

1 tablespoon extra-virgin olive oil, for frying

8 to 10 small flour tortillas

Pickled Red Onions (page 207)

2 avocados, sliced

Fresh cilantro

1 cup cotija cheese

Lime wedges

These fish tacos are a fabulous option for hosting and entertaining. They are fresh, beautiful, and delicious, and I just love serving them up with bright, fresh, seasonal garnishes.

In a large, flat bowl, combine the paprika, chili powder, cayenne pepper, and salt.

Pat the fish fillets dry with paper towels and then cut the fish into 1- to 2-inch strips. Dredge the fish strips through the seasoning mix to coat on both sides.

In a medium or large cast-iron skillet, heat the oil. Place each piece of fish in oil and panfry, approximately 4 minutes on each side, or until golden brown and fully cooked in the center. Place the fish pieces on a paper towel–lined plate or rack to let excess oil drain off.

To assemble the tacos, place the fried fish on tortillas. Layer on Pickled Red Onions, avocado, cilantro, and cotija cheese. Finish off with a squeeze of fresh lime juice.

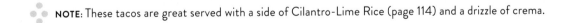 **NOTE:** These tacos are great served with a side of Cilantro-Lime Rice (page 114) and a drizzle of crema.

Mussels in White Wine–Butter Sauce

4 tablespoon butter, plus more for buttering baguette slices

3 green onions, finely sliced

6 garlic cloves, minced

6 thyme sprigs

3 pounds mussels, debearded, scrubbed, and rinsed

1½ cups heavy cream

1¼ cups dry white wine

⅓ cup chopped fresh Italian parsley

Kosher salt, to taste

Freshly ground black pepper, to taste

1 French bread baguette, for serving

These mussels are a delicious and surprisingly simple meal that will transport you to your favorite coast. Being able to make these mussels at home is both an adventure and a treat.

In a large pot or Dutch oven over medium heat, melt the butter, then increase the heat to high and add the green onions, garlic, and thyme. Sauté for 1 to 2 minutes.

Add the mussels to the butter mixture and cover, steaming for 6 to 8 minutes or until the mussels pop open. Discard any that remain unopened.

Remove the thyme sprigs and discard. Pour in the cream and white wine. Add the parsley and season with salt and pepper. Mix together gently and remove from the heat.

Cut the baguette into angled slices and lightly butter, toasting on a dry skillet until the bread is slightly charred.

Enjoy a slice or two of baguette with your bowl of steamed mussels—it's perfect for dipping in the white wine–butter sauce.

St. George Island Shrimp and Grits

SERVES 6

3 tablespoons butter

1 tablespoon minced garlic

1 pound shrimp, peeled and deveined

Juice of ¼ lemon

Salt, to taste

Freshly ground black pepper, to taste

1 recipe Sweet Corn and Cheese Grits (page 110)

The beach I grew up going to is on the Forgotten Coast of Florida, a place called St. George Island. We'd get shrimp fresh off the boat, come home after a day at the beach, and cook it for a delicious meal. This recipe is how I fix it up in my kitchen, balancing the traditional ingredients with a punch of flavor.

In a large skillet over low to medium heat, melt the butter and add the garlic. Once the garlic is hot, 2 to 3 minutes, add the shrimp and cook until pink, 3 to 5 minutes. When the shrimp is finished cooking, season with lemon juice, salt, and pepper.

Spoon cheese grits into individual serving bowls and place shrimp on top. Serve immediately.

Low-Country Boil

SERVES 10

½ cup Old Bay Seasoning

4 pounds medium red potatoes

2 yellow onions, cut in chunks

2½ pounds cured, smoked pork sausage links, cut into 3-inch pieces

8 ears of corn, cut in half

4 pounds medium shrimp

Try this fun one-pot meal for your next get-together. Lay down last week's newspaper pages on the table, pour the Low-Country Boil right on top, and have a roll of paper towels handy as you dig in. We love enjoying a boil for dinner while we're at the beach, with fresh shrimp right off the boat. It's great for a crowd.

Fill a 7-gallon stockpot halfway with water (or use 2 large pots and divide the ingredients between them). Add the Old Bay and bring to a rolling boil.

Add the whole potatoes to the pot. Allow the water to return to a boil and cook for 5 minutes. Add the onions and sausage. Bring the water back to a boil and cook for 15 minutes.

Add the corn. Bring the water back to a boil and cook for 10 minutes, or until the potatoes are tender. Add the shrimp. Bring the water back to a boil and cook until the shrimp turn pink, about 3 more minutes.

Drain everything through a colander, discard the liquid, and serve on a layer of newspaper spread out on the table.

Sunday Pot Roast with Gravy

SERVES 6 TO 8

FOR THE POT ROAST

1 tablespoon extra-virgin olive oil

1 tablespoon butter

3 garlic cloves, minced

1 (1½-pound) roast

Kosher salt, to taste

Freshly ground black pepper, to taste

1 medium yellow onion, quartered

4 to 6 carrots, peeled and cut into 2- to 3-inch lengths

1 bundle fresh thyme

10 to 12 small white potatoes, quartered

FOR THE GRAVY

Drippings from roast

2 to 4 tablespoons flour

½ to 1 cup water

⅛ teaspoon Kitchen Bouquet Browning and Seasoning Sauce

Sunday Pot Roast with Gravy is one of my favorite timeless meals that Mom would make many a Sunday afternoon. Best when slow-cooked on a slow day, its aroma completely fills the house and your whole family can gather around for dinner.

Preheat the oven to 350 degrees F.

To make the pot roast, in a large cast-iron skillet or Dutch oven, heat the olive oil and butter on the stovetop. Lightly sauté the garlic until it just begins to brown, then add the roast. Sear the meat until browned on all sides. Season with salt and pepper, and remove the pan from the heat.

Scatter the onion, carrots, and thyme around the roast. Cover, place in the oven, and cook for 3 hours. Remove the pan from the oven and add the quartered potatoes around the roast, rolling and coating them in the drippings from the roast for flavor. Cover the pan, return to the oven, and roast for another 45 minutes to 1 hour, until the potatoes are tender and the meat is fully cooked. The meat should fall apart on the fork.

To make the gravy, remove the vegetables and roast from the pan to a serving platter. Scrape the bottom of the pan with a wooden spoon. Add the flour to the drippings and stir over low heat to create a stiff roux mixture. Slowly add water to reach the desired gravy consistency (similar to heavy cream). Continue to stir over a low heat. Add a splash of Kitchen Bouquet for color and flavor.

NOTE: For the perfect gravy, see How to Make a Roux (page 21). Remember to not add more flour once you have already added water to the mixture or you'll end up with lumpy gravy.

—◦· **HIGHLIGHTS** ·◦—

Sunday Pot Roast with Gravy is one of my go-to Dutch oven recipes.

Shrimp Scampi with Linguine Pasta

SERVES 4 TO 8

1 (16-ounce) package linguine pasta

4 tablespoons butter, divided

5 tablespoons extra-virgin olive oil, divided

2 shallots, finely diced

1 tablespoon minced garlic

¼ tablespoon red pepper flakes

1 pound shrimp, peeled and deveined

Kosher salt, to taste

Freshly ground black pepper, to taste

½ cup dry white wine

Juice of 1 lemon

Grated Parmigiano Reggiano cheese, for topping

¼ cup finely chopped fresh parsley leaves or sprig of fresh thyme, for garnishing

This flavor-filled pasta dish is one I love to make for a crowd—it's nothing short of delicious.

Bring a large pot of salted water to a boil and cook the pasta for about 8 minutes.

In a large skillet over medium heat, melt 2 tablespoons of butter with 2 tablespoons of oil. Add the shallots, garlic, and red pepper flakes. Sauté for about 4 minutes, until the shallots are tender.

Season the shrimp with salt and black pepper and add to skillet. Cook until the shrimp are pink, about 3 minutes. Remove the shrimp from the pan.

Add the white wine and lemon juice to the skillet mixture. Bring to a boil, scraping any brown bits from the bottom of the pan to keep it from burning.

Add the remaining 2 tablespoons of butter and 2 tablespoons oil to the skillet; bring the mixture to a simmer.

Add the shrimp back into the skillet and season with salt and black pepper. Add the remaining 1 tablespoon of olive oil if needed to reach the desired consistency.

Top with cheese and garnish with chopped parsley to serve.

Mom's Spaghetti and Meatballs

SERVES 6

1 pound ground beef

¼ pound ground pork

⅓ cup bread crumbs

¼ teaspoon dried oregano

¼ cup finely chopped parsley

1 cup freshly grated Parmesan cheese, plus more for serving

1 large egg

3 garlic cloves, minced

1 teaspoon kosher salt, plus more to taste

2 tablespoons extra-virgin olive oil

½ cup finely chopped onion

½ cup finely chopped celery

2 (28-ounce) cans crushed tomatoes

1 (6-ounce) can tomato paste

2 bay leaves

Freshly ground black pepper, to taste

1 (16-ounce) package spaghetti

Fresh basil, for serving

Spaghetti and meatballs is a classic, and I can name a few families I know off the top of my head who eat this dish once a week. This tried-and-true recipe is a staple in the home for a reason. Here's our family's rendition.

In a large bowl, combine the beef and pork with the bread crumbs, oregano, parsley, Parmesan cheese, egg, garlic, and 1 teaspoon salt. Mix until combined, then form into 1½-inch balls.

In a large pot or Dutch oven over medium heat, heat the oil. Add the meatballs and cook, turning occasionally, until browned on all sides, about 10 minutes. Transfer the meatballs to a plate.

Add the onion and celery to the pot and cook until soft, about 5 minutes. Add the crushed tomatoes, tomato paste, and bay leaves. Season with salt and pepper and bring to a simmer. Return the meatballs to pot and cover. Simmer until the sauce has thickened, 8 to 10 minutes.

While the meatballs are cooking, in a large pot of salted boiling water, cook pasta until al dente. Drain.

Serve pasta with a scoop of sauce and meatballs on top. Top with extra Parmesan and fresh basil before serving.

Garlic-Roasted Whole Chicken with Cayenne

SERVES 6

1 (4- to 5-pound) whole chicken, room temperature, giblets discarded

6 tablespoons unsalted butter, softened, divided

1 bundle fresh rosemary

8 to 10 garlic cloves, 4 minced and 4 to 6 smashed

1/4 teaspoon cayenne pepper

Kosher salt, to taste

Freshly ground black pepper, to taste

1 lemon, sliced

2 onions, quartered

There is nothing better than a hot, roasted chicken with flavorful, crispy skin. It is similar to the rotisserie chicken you can get at the grocery store, but so much better homemade—like most things. It's an impressive, yet relatively simple hearty dish to add to your rotation.

Position the rack in the lower third of the oven and preheat to 425 degrees F.

Pat the chicken dry and rub half of the butter all over the chicken.

Set aside 2 whole rosemary sprigs and mince the remaining rosemary. Rub the minced rosemary and minced garlic all over the chicken, and then season with the cayenne pepper, salt, and black pepper.

Generously season the cavity of chicken with salt and black pepper, and then stuff with most of the lemon slices, 2 to 4 cloves of smashed garlic, and 2 or 3 quarters of onion. Truss the chicken legs with cooking twine and tuck the wings under the bird.

Place the chicken in a roasting pan, breast-side up, and surround with any remaining onion quarters, smashed garlic, lemon slices, and the 2 whole rosemary sprigs. Roast for 25 minutes and then baste with juices. Roast another 25 to 30 minutes, until the skin is lightly browned. Continue to roast for 15 to 20 minutes more, or until a meat thermometer reaches 155 to 160 degrees F as measured on the thickest part of the thigh, and juices are running clear. Allow the chicken to rest for 15 minutes and carve to serve.

Beefsteak Tomato Sandwiches with Mayo

MAKES 3 SANDWICHES

1 large beefsteak tomato

2 to 4 tablespoons Homemade Mayo (page 205) or mayonnaise of choice

6 slices white bread

Kosher salt, to taste

Freshly ground black pepper, to taste

Nothing beats a classic tomato sandwich with fresh tomatoes from your garden during the summertime. I cannot get enough of these sandwiches.

Slice the tomato into medium-thick slices and set aside.

Generously spread mayonnaise onto each slice of bread. Layer tomato slices onto a single slice of bread and sprinkle generously with salt and pepper.

Add the final slice of bread on top to make your sandwich.

Weeknight Veggie Pasta

SERVES 8

1 (16-ounce) package angel hair pasta

1 pound fresh asparagus, trimmed

3 handfuls sugar snap peas, trimmed

¼ cup extra-virgin olive oil

Lemon zest, to taste

Fresh lemon juice

Kosher salt, to taste

Freshly ground black pepper, to taste

½ cup grated or shaved Parmigiano Reggiano cheese

The easiest, and most delicious, way to sneak fresh veggies into a meal for your kids is in a veggie pasta. This fresh and light recipe is great for whatever seasonal vegetables you find at the market. Top with fresh lemon zest and Parmigiano Reggiano cheese for a bright and simple way to bring out the flavor.

In a large pot of salted boiling water, cook the pasta until al dente, 3 to 5 minutes. Add in the asparagus and sugar snap peas and cook for another 3 minutes, or until tender. Drain and set aside.

Toss the hot noodles in a light drizzle of olive oil and toss with peas and asparagus.

To serve, use tongs to spin pasta into bird's nest piles, drizzle with a bit more olive oil, add lemon zest and a squeeze of fresh juice, and season with salt and pepper. Finish with a hearty sprinkling of Parmigiano Reggiano on top.

⋅❖⋅ HIGHLIGHTS ⋅❖⋅

Need protein in your meal? Swap your regular pasta for a chickpea variation, or add grilled chicken breast or shrimp to complete the meal.

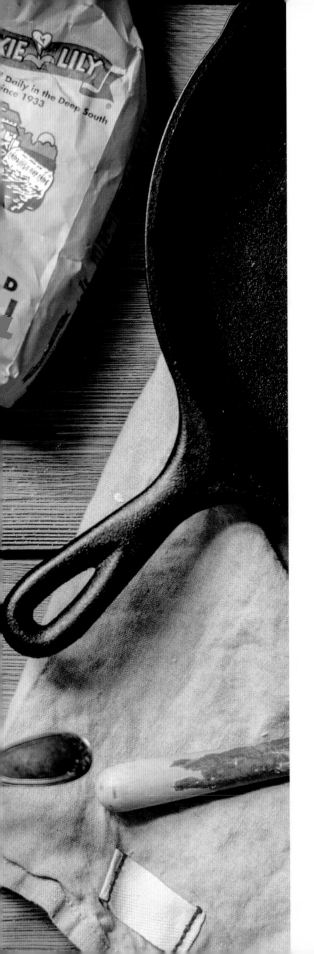

SIDE DISHES

.·—·.

While some may believe the
entrée is the hero of any meal;
I may beg to differ. I'd fight
hard for the case that a rotation
of a few fabulous sides are
the real winners. When perfected,
they can truly make the meal
experience one to remember.

Cast-Iron Sautéed Brussels Sprouts

SERVES 4 TO 6

1 pint Brussels sprouts

1 to 2 tablespoons extra-virgin olive oil

Kosher salt, to taste

¼ cup shredded Parmigiano Reggiano cheese

We are addicted to Brussels sprouts in our house and have made them every which way. These roasted Brussels sprouts are foolproof, and so very tasty.

Preheat oven to 375 degrees F.

Trim the bottoms off of the Brussels sprouts, and slice each in half top to bottom. In a large cast-iron skillet over medium-high heat, heat the oil until it shimmers. Put the Brussels sprouts, cut-side down, in one layer in the skillet. Sprinkle with salt.

Cook, undisturbed, until the Brussels sprouts begin to brown on the bottom, then transfer the skillet to the oven. Roast, shaking the skillet every 5 minutes, until the Brussels sprouts are quite brown and tender, 10 to 20 minutes depending on the size of the Brussels sprouts. Toss with shredded Parmigiano Reggiano for a salty finish.

NOTE: We photographed this recipe on the same day we made Homemade Mayo (page 205). Add a dollop to your finished Brussels sprouts and I can promise you there won't be a sprout left in the bowl when the meal is over.

Collard Greens with Applewood Bacon

SERVES 6 TO 8

6 strips thick-sliced applewood bacon, cut into ½-inch pieces

1 small yellow onion, chopped

2 garlic cloves, minced

¼ cup apple-cider vinegar

2 pounds fresh collard greens, stems removed and sliced into 3-inch-wide strips

1 cup chicken broth

1 teaspoon kosher salt

½ teaspoon freshly ground black pepper

A TRADITIONAL SIDE DISH for your New Year's Day menu, collards are said to bring wealth and prosperity in the new year.

When we drive home from the family farm, we always pass a homemade sign reading simply: GREENS. Collard greens are a Southern staple for the table. The acidity from vinegar and grease from the bacon perfectly balance the bitterness of the collards themselves.

In a large skillet over medium-low heat, cook the bacon for 8 to 12 minutes, turning over once, until desired crispness. Remove bacon and roughly chop; set aside. Sauté the onion and garlic in bacon grease for several minutes over low heat until the onion begins to soften. Add the vinegar and allow the mixture to cook until the liquid has reduced by about half. Add the collard greens, chicken broth, salt, and pepper and bring to a simmer at medium-low heat. Stir the mixture occasionally, until the collard greens have wilted and lost their brightness.

Serve warm with juices from the pan.

Day Pickles in a Jar

½ cup water

½ cup white vinegar

1 tablespoon kosher salt

1 to 2 cucumbers, thinly sliced with skin on

1 to 2 celery stalks, sliced

2 to 3 small spring onions, quartered

1 small green tomato, sliced

1 jalapeño, seeded and sliced

2 to 3 radishes, quartered

2 garlic cloves, smashed

1 bundle onion flowers, dill flowers, or parsley flowers

Our day-pickle recipe is easy and can be accomplished in just a short amount of time compared to a true pickling and preserving tactic. Growing up with a garden where cukes were plentiful, the "quick pickle" was always the summertime vegetable preserving method we were certain to enjoy.

In a glass measuring cup, make a brine by combining the water, vinegar, and salt.

Tightly pack a 1-pint jar with the cucumbers, celery, onions, tomato, jalapeño, radishes, garlic, and herb flowers.

Pour the brine mixture over the ingredients in the jar. The vegetables should be completely immersed in the brine. Since these refrigerator pickles will not be canned, it is not necessary to leave head space between the surface of the food and the rims of the jars.

Fasten the lid onto the jar and store in the refrigerator for at least 24 hours before eating. Keeps up to 7 days in the refrigerator.

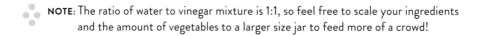 **NOTE:** The ratio of water to vinegar mixture is 1:1, so feel free to scale your ingredients and the amount of vegetables to a larger size jar to feed more of a crowd!

Cornmeal-Fried Okra

SERVES 12

1 pound okra

1½ cups Made-from-Scratch Buttermilk (page 211), or buttermilk of choice

¾ cup all-purpose flour of choice

1 cup Dixie Lily cornmeal, or cornmeal of choice

½ teaspoon cayenne pepper

Canola or vegetable oil, for frying

Kosher salt, to taste

This salty and crunchy okra is everything you could dream of and more. Its crispy, fried breading and soft inside is hard to say no to.

Rinse the okra in cold water for approximately 5 minutes. Chop the okra into bite-size pieces and soak in bowl of buttermilk for 10 minutes.

While the okra is soaking, combine the flour, cornmeal, and cayenne in a large bowl. When the okra is ready, toss the pieces of buttermilk-soaked okra in the flour mixture until all sides are well coated.

In a large cast-iron skillet over medium heat, heat approximately 1½ inches of oil until tiny bubbles form on the handle of a wooden spoon dipped into the oil.

Carefully place the okra in the hot oil and allow to brown on one side before turning to brown on the other, 2 to 3 minutes per side.

Remove the okra with a slotted spoon or spatula and place on a paper towel–lined baking sheet to soak up any excess grease. Immediately sprinkle generously with kosher salt while still hot.

Sweet Corn and Cheese Grits

SERVES 6 TO 8

1 tablespoon extra-virgin
olive oil

1/2 sweet onion, diced

1 garlic clove, minced

1/2 cup sweet corn kernels

1 cup heavy cream

3 cups chicken stock

1 cup stone-ground grits

1 teaspoon coarse-ground salt,
plus more to taste

Freshly ground black pepper,
to taste

1/4 cup shredded cheddar
cheese

1 tablespoon unsalted butter

Grits are a staple in any Southern home. Growing up, we all learn how to make grits, and everyone has their own special way. I promise you this is the best grits recipe out there, with a simple secret ingredient that makes them so creamy.

In a large saucepan over medium heat, heat the oil. Add the onion and garlic and cook until transparent, about 2 minutes. Add corn kernels and cook an additional 2 to 4 minutes, until tender.

Increase the heat to medium-high; add the cream and chicken stock. Bring the mixture to a boil and whisk in the grits. Season with salt and pepper.

Reduce the heat to low and simmer, stirring often, until the grits are tender and creamy, 45 to 60 minutes. Mix in the cheddar cheese and butter, and adjust for seasoning with salt and pepper. Serve immediately.

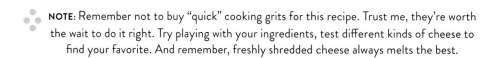

NOTE: Remember not to buy "quick" cooking grits for this recipe. Trust me, they're worth the wait to do it right. Try playing with your ingredients, test different kinds of cheese to find your favorite. And remember, freshly shredded cheese always melts the best.

111

Aunt Carol's Macaroni and Cheese

SERVES 8 TO 12

1/2 cup butter

1/2 cup all-purpose flour

1/2 teaspoon salt

1/2 teaspoon freshly ground black pepper

1/4 teaspoon cayenne pepper

1/4 teaspoon garlic powder

2 cups fat-free half-and-half

2 cups milk

2 (8-ounce) blocks sharp cheddar cheese, shredded

1 (8-ounce) block extra-sharp cheddar cheese, shredded

1 (16-ounce) package elbow macaroni, cooked

If you're looking for a creamy, authentic Southern macaroni and cheese, then this is for you. Aunt Carol's recipe has been a staple at family gatherings at the farm for years. It's the perfect blend of both a creamy and baked macaroni and cheese.

Preheat the oven to 350 degrees F, and grease a 9 x 13-inch baking dish.

In a large skillet over medium-high heat, melt the butter. Gradually whisk in the flour until the mixture is smooth. Cook, whisking constantly, for 2 minutes.

Stir in the salt, black pepper, cayenne pepper, and garlic powder. Gradually whisk in the half-and-half and milk. Cook, whisking constantly, for 8 to 10 minutes, or until thickened.

Stir in half of the sharp cheddar cheese and all of the extra-sharp cheddar cheese until the mixture is smooth. Remove from the heat and combine the macaroni with the cheese sauce.

Pour the mixture into the prepared baking dish, and sprinkle with the remaining 4 ounces of sharp cheddar cheese. Bake for 20 to 25 minutes, until the cheese is bubbly and slightly browned.

Cilantro-Lime Rice

MAKES 4 TO 6 CUPS

1 tablespoon extra-virgin olive oil

2 garlic cloves, minced

2 cups uncooked basmati or long-grain white rice

4 cups water

1 teaspoon kosher salt

Zest of 1 lime

Juice of 1 lime

¾ cup chopped cilantro

This recipe came about as an easy, flavorful alternative to plain white rice. A few fresh squeezes of lime make just about anything better, and this combo is bright and delicious.

In a large saucepan over medium heat, heat the oil and sauté the garlic, stirring constantly for 2 minutes to bring out the flavor. Stir in the rice.

Add the water and salt, raise the heat to high, and bring to a boil. Cover and reduce the heat to a simmer; cook for 12 to 15 minutes, until the rice is tender and the water has been absorbed.

Remove from the heat and stir in lime zest and juice. Fold in the cilantro and serve.

Sesame Fried Rice

SERVES 6

2 cups uncooked basmati rice

2 large eggs

1 tablespoon minced garlic

3 tablespoons extra-virgin olive oil

1/4 tablespoon sesame oil

1/4 tablespoon low-sodium soy sauce

1 tablespoon sesame seeds, for serving

1 cup sliced green onions, for serving

A spin on our favorite hibachi-style rice, this dish makes a wonderful side or base when paired with chicken, shrimp, or fish. The savory flavors of the sesame, green onions, and soy sauce provide a rich profile you're sure to love.

In a medium saucepan, cook basmati rice according to package directions until tender and water has been absorbed, approximately 15 minutes.

In a large frying pan over medium heat, scramble the eggs and minced garlic in the oil. Add in the cooked rice, sesame oil, and soy sauce.

Once well combined, spoon fried-rice mixture into a serving bowl. Toss in sesame seeds and green onions to serve.

NOTE: To mix it up and get in more veggies, add in a variety of chopped, stir-fried vegetables. Try asparagus, peas, bell peppers, broccoli, or other favorites.

Roasted Vegetables

SERVES 4 TO 6

4 to 5 cups vegetables (such as mushrooms, okra, Brussels sprouts, peppers, and so on), chopped into bite-size pieces or slices

2 tablespoons extra-virgin olive oil

1 teaspoon kosher salt

¼ cup shredded Parmigiano Reggiano cheese

Like many parents, I often struggle with getting my little ones to enjoy eating a variety of vegetables. That's why I love this recipe for roasted veggies. It's simple and turns everything from mushrooms to okra into a delicious meal that even my kids will eat.

Preheat the oven to 375 degrees F.

Spread the vegetables on a baking sheet.

Drizzle the vegetables with olive oil and sprinkle salt and Parmigiano Reggiano cheese over the top.

Roast in oven for 20 to 30 minutes, flipping halfway through the cooking time. I like mine super crispy (okay, nearly burnt!), so I tend to leave mine in on the longer side.

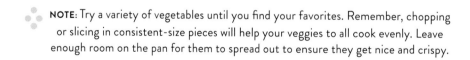

NOTE: Try a variety of vegetables until you find your favorites. Remember, chopping or slicing in consistent-size pieces will help your veggies to all cook evenly. Leave enough room on the pan for them to spread out to ensure they get nice and crispy.

Parker House Rolls

1¼ cups whole milk

½ cup unsalted butter, cut into small cubes, plus more for serving

½ cup sugar

1 package active dry yeast

½ cup warm water

3 large eggs, lightly beaten

2 teaspoons kosher salt, plus more for serving

6 cups all-purpose flour, plus more for flouring

A warm, soft roll is always a lovely addition to a family supper.

In a small saucepan over low heat, bring the milk to a simmer. Remove the saucepan from the heat and stir in the cubed butter and sugar. Let cool.

In a small bowl, dissolve the yeast into the warm water. Please note: The water needs to be warm but not too hot for the yeast to properly dissolve. Let set until foamy, about 5 minutes.

In a stand mixer with a dough attachment, combine the milk mixture, eggs, yeast mixture, salt, and ½ of the flour. Mix until smooth. Add the remaining flour, ½ cup at a time, mixing until a smooth ball forms.

On a floured surface, knead the dough by hand for about 7 minutes. Place the dough in a greased bowl, cover, and let rise for about 1 hour and 5 minutes.

On a floured surface, punch down the dough and shape into 24 (1-inch) balls. Place the dough balls on a baking sheet lined with parchment paper approximately 2 inches apart, cover, and let rise for about 35 minutes.

Preheat the oven to 350 degrees F.

Bake the rolls for about 20 minutes, or until the rolls are a nice, golden brown. Remove from the oven and use a pastry brush to cover each roll with butter. Lightly salt before serving.

Skillet Cornbread with Leeks

SERVES 8 TO 10

1½ cups yellow cornmeal

1 cup all-purpose flour

1½ teaspoons baking powder

½ teaspoon baking soda

1¼ teaspoons kosher salt

2 green leeks, thinly sliced

1¾ cups buttermilk

1 large egg

4 tablespoons unsalted butter, cut into 4 pieces

1 bundle fresh chives, chopped

This crispy-yet-fluffy cornbread goes the extra mile to be more than your average cornbread. The leeks pack a mighty punch of flavor.

Preheat the oven to 425 degrees F.

In a large bowl, whisk together the cornmeal, flour, baking powder, baking soda, salt, and leeks.

In a large measuring cup, whisk together the buttermilk and the egg. Pour the buttermilk mixture into the dry ingredients and stir the batter together until completely combined.

Put the butter in a 10-inch cast-iron skillet and place in oven for 3 to 5 minutes to melt the butter.

Remove the skillet from the oven, swirl the butter around to coat the bottom and sides, then pour the batter into the prepared skillet. Smooth the top and bake 20 to 25 minutes. Serve warm.

NOTE: Try this with some of our Honey Butter (page 214) or Fresh Herb Butter (page 214) for even more flavor.

Cast-Iron Rosemary Bread

SERVES 8 TO 10

1 package active dry yeast

2 cups lukewarm water

1 pinch of sugar

4 1/3 cups all-purpose flour, plus more for flouring

1 1/2 teaspoons kosher salt, plus more to taste

Extra-virgin olive oil, for the skillet and for garnishing

Rosemary leaves, for garnishing

This homemade cast-iron skillet bread is the perfect recipe to keep you warm and cozy. It is especially delish topped with Homemade Butter (page 212) and honey.

In a large mixing bowl, combine the yeast, warm water, and pinch of sugar. Let set for 5 to 10 minutes to activate. Add in 1 cup of the flour and 1 1/2 teaspoons of salt and use a wooden spoon to mix until combined. Stir in the rest of the flour, 1 cup at a time, until it is completely mixed. Cover the bowl with plastic wrap and allow to rise for 1 hour or until double in size.

Lightly oil the bottom of a 10- or 12-inch skillet. Sprinkle the dough with flour; flour your hands as well. Do not punch down the dough. Shape the dough into a disk—it will be sticky. Place in the skillet and cover loosely with a tea towel. Allow the dough to rise for another 30 minutes.

Preheat the oven to 400 degrees F.

Drizzle a little more olive oil over the top of the bread and cut an X shape into the dough. Fill this X with rosemary and a sprinkle of salt. Bake for 35 to 40 minutes, until the top of the bread is a deep brown color.

COOKIES, CANDIES & TREATS

•⁃——⁃•

Growing up we always had a homemade sweet treat thanks to Mom. There is just something so nostalgic about homemade sweets. Here are a few go-to recipes you should try.

Vintage Glass–Stamped Cookies

MAKES 12 COOKIES

2 3/4 cups all-purpose flour, plus more

1 teaspoon baking soda

1/2 teaspoon baking powder

1 cup butter, room temperature

1 1/2 cups sugar

1 teaspoon vanilla extract

1 large egg

BEFORE YOU MAKE
the cookie dough, you'll need to find the perfect glass with a decorative bottom design for inspiration. Bring the kids along and turn it into a fun family outing, letting everyone pick out their own pretty glass. Thrift stores, Goodwill, or antique malls are the perfect place to look. They usually have an abundance of discarded glasses looking for a new home and most can be found at a great price.

This is a fun twist on a classic sugar cookie, because sometimes doing things the old-fashioned way is more fun. Much like folks used to use tin cans as a biscuit cutter, we're making beautiful stamped designs using vintage glassware.

In a small bowl, combine the flour, baking soda, and baking powder.

Using a stand mixer, cream the butter and sugar until smooth. Gradually beat in the vanilla and the egg.

Slowly add the flour mixture to the butter mixture, and stir until combined. Form the dough into a log, wrap in waxed paper, and chill in the refrigerator for at least 2 hours.

Preheat the oven to 350 degrees F. Grease a baking sheet.

Remove the dough from the refrigerator, unwrap, and slice rounds approximately 1/4 inch thick. Place the rounds on the baking sheet, leaving about 2 inches between them.

Choose a vintage glass or two with a crystal-cut design on the bottom that you like. Dip the bottom of the glasses in flour so they don't stick to the dough. Stamp the cookies with the glasses by lightly pressing the bottom of the glass into the top of each cookie dough slice.

Bake for 8 to 10 minutes, or until cookies just begin to turn golden in color. Remove from the oven, let the cookies cool on the baking sheet for 2 minutes, and then transfer to a wire rack to completely cool before serving.

Cookies, Candies & Treats

Toffee Bars

MAKES 16 TO 24 BARS

FOR THE CRUST

1/2 cup butter

1/2 cup sugar

1/2 teaspoon salt

1 cup all-purpose flour

FOR THE FILLING

1 (14-ounce) can sweetened condensed milk

2 tablespoons butter

1/4 teaspoon salt

2 teaspoons vanilla extract

FOR THE FROSTING

1 ounce unsweetened chocolate

2 tablespoons butter

1 1/2 cups sugar

1 teaspoon vanilla extract

2 tablespoons hot water

These Toffee Bars have a buttery crust followed by a gooey toffee layer and then a crisp little chocolate layer to top it all off. I love cutting them on the small side so they're perfectly bite-size, and I often add a pinch more kosher salt than the recipe calls for because I love that salty and sweet balance.

Preheat oven to 350 degrees F. Grease a 9 x 13-inch pan.

To make the crust, in a medium bowl, cream the butter, sugar, and salt together. Mix in the flour to combine. Pat the mixture into the prepared pan. Bake for 15 minutes or until light brown. Remove from the oven.

While crust is baking, make the filling. In a small saucepan over medium heat, stir together the condensed milk, butter, and salt until the butter melts. Cook over medium heat for 5 minutes, stirring, until mixture thickens and becomes smooth. Stir in the vanilla.

Spread the filling mixture over the baked crust. Return to the oven and bake for 12 to 15 minutes, or until golden. The bars are better when this layer is just slightly undercooked.

To make the frosting, in a clean saucepan over medium heat, melt the chocolate and butter. Add the sugar and vanilla. Stir in the hot water and blend together.

Spread the frosting over the filling while still warm and cut into bars.

Soft Peanut Butter Cookies

MAKES 24 COOKIES

½ cup shortening

½ cup peanut butter

½ cup sugar

½ cup packed brown sugar

1 large egg

1¼ cups all-purpose flour

½ teaspoon baking powder

¾ teaspoon baking soda

¼ teaspoon salt

These chewy, nutty cookies are undeniably a favorite.

Preheat the oven to 375 degrees F, and lightly grease a baking sheet.

In a large bowl, mix the shortening, peanut butter, sugar, brown sugar, and egg together until well combined.

In a medium bowl, mix the flour, baking powder, baking soda, and salt together. Add the dry ingredients to the peanut butter mixture and thoroughly combine.

Roll the dough into 1¼-inch balls. Place balls 3 inches apart on the prepared baking sheet. Flatten each ball in a crisscross style with a floured fork.

Bake for 8 to 10 minutes. Let cool on the baking sheet for 2 minutes; transfer to wire racks to cool completely.

NOTE: I always underbake peanut butter cookies because I prefer them soft and falling apart in my mouth. Keep a close watch on these in the oven and take them out just as they start to brown. Remove them from the pan immediately to stop the baking process.

Chocolate Chip Cookies

MAKES 12 COOKIES

2¼ cups all-purpose flour

1 teaspoon baking soda

1 teaspoon salt

1 cup butter, room temperature

¾ cup sugar

¾ cup packed brown sugar

1 teaspoon vanilla extract

2 large eggs

2 cups semisweet chocolate chips

Buttery, rich, and gooey, these chocolate chip cookies are a timeless treat, and are best when served with a frosty glass of milk.

Preheat the oven to 375 degrees F.

In a small bowl, combine the flour, baking soda, and salt.

In a large bowl, beat the butter, sugar, brown sugar, and vanilla until creamy. Add the eggs, one at a time, beating well after each addition. Gradually beat in the flour mixture.

Stir in the chocolate chips. Drop by rounded tablespoons onto ungreased baking sheets.

Bake for 9 to 11 minutes or until golden brown. Let cool on the baking sheets for 2 minutes; transfer to wire racks to cool completely.

Banana Pudding Cups

SERVES 8

1 (5-ounce) box vanilla instant pudding

2 cups milk

1 (14-ounce) can sweetened condensed milk

1 tablespoon vanilla extract

Homemade Whipped Cream (page 160)

Vanilla wafer cookies, as needed

3 to 4 ripe bananas, sliced

NOTE: This is a wonderful recipe to double and feed a crowd. Simply layer it into a glass baking dish for a pretty presentation that's easy to assemble and serve.

These pudding cups will bring back fond memories of your childhood. They're also a great use for those overripe bananas you have on hand. Homemade whipped cream to top it off makes all the difference.

In a large bowl, stir together the vanilla pudding mix and milk. Stir in the condensed milk and vanilla extract until smooth.

Gently fold in the whipped cream. Do not overmix; you want to maintain the light, whipped feeling of the mixture.

In eight individual serving dishes, layer vanilla wafer cookies, banana slices, and pudding mix. Repeat layers until all the ingredients are used. Top with a few crumbled-up cookies and a fresh banana slice. Keep this pudding in the refrigerator until serving.

Meringue with Fresh Berries

SERVES 8

3 egg whites, room temperature

1 teaspoon vanilla extract

¼ teaspoon cream of tartar

Dash of salt

1 cup sugar

Homemade Whipped Cream (page 160)

4 cups fresh berries, of choice

I have a laundry list of desserts that I claim as my "favorite," but meringue may be at the top. Growing up in humid Florida, there weren't many days when the weather was perfect for making meringue and having it set up properly. It was a rare treat. Making meringue is a tradition I plan to share with my kids to pass down for another generation.

Preheat the oven to 275 degrees F.

Using a stand mixer, mix together the egg whites, vanilla, cream of tartar, and salt. Beat on medium-low speed until soft peaks form, approximately 8 minutes. Gradually add the sugar, beating until very stiff peaks form and the sugar is dissolved. The meringue will look glossy.

Line a baking sheet with plain, ungreased brown paper. Place 8 dollops of meringue onto the paper, trying to keep each dollop approximately the same size and spaced at least 1 inch a part. This allows for even baking. Using the back of a spoon, shape the meringue into shells, about ½ inch thick and about 1¾ inches high.

Bake for about 1 hour. Keeping the over door shut, turn off the heat, and let the meringues dry in the oven for at least 2 hours.

Top with whipped cream and fresh berries to serve.

NOTE: Meringues are delicious on their own and simply melt in your mouth. They pair well with many kinds of fresh fruit and a spoonful of whipped cream. Instead of making small, individual meringue shells, try your hand at making one larger shell to serve a crowd. It looks impressive and makes for a beautiful centerpiece on the table.

Nostalgic Whoopie Pies

MAKES 6 WHOOPIE PIES

FOR THE PIES

1 cup packed dark brown sugar

½ cup shortening

1 large egg

2 cups all-purpose flour

¼ cup unsweetened cocoa powder

1 teaspoon baking powder

1 teaspoon baking soda

1 teaspoon salt

1 cup milk

1 teaspoon vanilla extract

FOR THE FILLING

2 cups marshmallow fluff

1½ cups powdered sugar

1 cup shortening

1 teaspoon vanilla extract

THE PRETTY TEXTURE of the marshmallow fluff mixture reminds me of my grandmother. She always had a jug of it in her pantry for some reason—fudge perhaps? Her pantry was always stocked full of baking goods, so she was able to make any and every recipe at a moment's notice without going to the store. My mom's pantry, and mine, are the same today.

There is nothing quite as nostalgic as a whoopie pie. Its classic look and sweet taste can transport you back in time—even if you never actually had one as a kid.

Preheat the oven to 350 degrees F. Grease a baking sheet and set aside.

To make the pies, in a stand mixer using the paddle attachment, cream the brown sugar, shortening, and egg together. In a separate bowl, mix together the flour, cocoa powder, baking powder, baking soda, and salt. Slowly add the dry mixture to the creamed mixture, ensuring they are well mixed. Slowly add in the milk and vanilla until the batter is well mixed.

Place spoonfuls of the batter onto the prepared baking sheet to make 12 pie halves, smoothing them to ensure each pie is as level as possible for even baking. Make sure you give enough space between each, as they will spread slightly during baking. Bake for 12 to 15 minutes.

Remove the pies from the oven and allow them to cool completely on a wire rack.

While pies are cooling, make the filling. Using a stand mixer with the whisk attachment, combine the marshmallow fluff, powdered sugar, and shortening. Add the vanilla and mix until well combined.

To assemble the Whoopie Pies, take one pie and spread it with a generous amount of filling. Take a second pie and press together to make a sandwich. Continue until all the pies are assembled.

Autumn Pear Crisp

FOR THE FILLING

6 Bosc pears

½ cup sugar

1 teaspoon ground cinnamon

1 teaspoon ground nutmeg

FOR THE CRISP TOPPING

¾ cup all-purpose flour

¾ cup old-fashioned rolled oats

¾ cup packed light brown sugar

1 teaspoon vanilla extract

¼ teaspoon salt

8 tablespoons chilled unsalted butter, cut into ½-inch pieces

1 tablespoon pure maple syrup

TO SERVE

Vanilla ice cream or Homemade Whipped Cream (page 160)

Drizzle of Sea Salt Caramel Sauce (page 154)

Topped with vanilla ice cream or freshly whipped cream, this pear crisp is superb for fall hosting.

Preheat the oven to 350 degrees F. Grease a 9 x 13-inch baking dish.

To make the filling, thinly slice the pears and discard the cores. In a large bowl mix the sugar, cinnamon, and nutmeg together, and then add the sliced pears. Gently toss to combine and to coat the pears. Spread the pear mixture into the prepared baking dish, and set aside.

To make the crisp topping, in a large mixing bowl, combine the flour, oats, brown sugar, vanilla, and salt and stir to combine evenly. Cut in the chilled butter pieces with a pastry blender or fork until the mixture forms clumps.

Scatter small clumps of topping over the pears to cover the entire surface and then drizzle with maple syrup.

Bake for 30 to 35 minutes, or until the topping is golden brown and the pear filling is bubbling. Remove from the oven and serve warm with a scoop of vanilla ice cream and a drizzle of caramel sauce.

Off-the-Vine Blackberry Crumble

SERVES 8

4 tablespoons sugar

4 cups fresh whole blackberries

2 cups all-purpose flour

2 cups old-fashioned rolled oats

1 cup packed light brown sugar

1 teaspoon ground cinnamon

1/2 teaspoon ground nutmeg

1 cup cold butter, cut into cubes, please extra for greasing

When I was growing up, there were woods next to our house and brambles of blackberry bushes would grow thick in the summertime. We'd stay outside and play all day long, popping over to the bush from time to time to pick a few juicy berries to enjoy. This blackberry crumble combines plump summer berries with a golden-brown crumbly crust to create the most magical summer dessert.

Preheat the oven to 350 degrees F, and grease a loaf pan with butter.

In a medium mixing bowl, combine the sugar with the blackberries to evenly coat the berries; set aside.

In a large mixing bowl, combine the flour, oats, brown sugar, cinnamon, and nutmeg. Cut in the butter with a pastry blender or fork until the mixture resembles gravel.

Add the sugared blackberries to the prepared baking dish in an even layer across the bottom. Top the berry mixture with the crumble crust mixture.

Bake for 45 minutes on center rack, until the crumble topping is golden brown.

Rustic Peach Cobbler

SERVES 6 TO 8

½ cup salted butter, melted, plus extra for greasing

4 peaches, sliced

1 cup sugar, divided, plus more for sprinkling

1 teaspoon vanilla extract

1 cup all-purpose flour

1 teaspoon baking powder

Ice cream of choice, optional

Peach cobbler is both simple and delicious—the perfect dessert to make for your friends and family, especially with a scoop of ice cream on top.

Preheat the oven to 350 degrees F. Grease a 9 x 13-inch baking dish with butter and set aside.

Mix the sliced peaches with ¼ cup sugar in the baking dish, and then spread evenly across the bottom of the dish.

In a medium bowl, mix together the remaining ¾ cup sugar, butter, vanilla, flour, and baking powder together into a dough. Drop clumps of this dough across the dish of peaches.

Sprinkle the cobbler with extra sugar, then bake for 40 to 50 minutes, or until dough is golden brown. Serve warm, alone or with a scoop of your favorite ice cream.

Cookies, Candies & Treats

Bourbon Bread Pudding

SERVES 8

1 cup raisins

1½ cups bourbon

2 cups whole milk

1 cup heavy cream

5 large eggs

½ cup sugar

1 teaspoon ground cinnamon

5 French bread rolls

I adore making Bourbon Bread Pudding, especially during holiday time. From the gooey, sweet center to the crispy edges, its flavor profile and taste make it a rich treat. The bourbon cuts the sweetness of this recipe just perfectly.

In a small bowl, soak the raisins in the bourbon for 1 hour.

Preheat the oven to 350 degrees F. Grease a 9 x 13-inch baking dish and set aside.

In a large mixing bowl, whisk together the milk, cream, eggs, sugar, and cinnamon. Add the soaked raisins and bourbon.

Tear the bread into large, bite-size pieces and place them in the prepared baking dish. Pour the cream mixture evenly across all of the bread pieces. Be sure to disperse the raisins throughout the dish.

Bake for 35 to 45 minutes, or until tops of bread are golden and liquid has set.

Let cool for 10 minutes, cut, and serve.

Pie Crust Cinnamon Rolls

MAKES 12 CINNAMON ROLLS

FOR THE PIE CRUST

1½ cups all-purpose flour, plus more for flouring

Dash of salt

¾ cup shortening

5 tablespoons cold water

FOR THE CINNAMON FILLING

3 tablespoons butter, melted

⅓ cup packed light brown sugar

2 teaspoons ground cinnamon

THIS IS MY MOM'S special recipe, which came about thanks to holiday pie baking. She would make Nana's Pie Crust (page 164) and have leftover scraps of dough, which she started rolling out to make these cinnamon rolls. I must say that I have come to love the rolls more than the pies themselves! This is the one recipe I always ask Mom to make and bring with her anytime she visits.

There is always one recipe you ask your mom to make when you're home or when she visits, and this is mine. Make these cinnamon rolls for dessert or a breakfast treat. We always enjoy these around the holidays.

Preheat the oven to 350 degrees F, and lightly grease a baking sheet.

To make the pie crust, in a mixing bowl, combine the flour and salt. Using a pastry blender, cut in the shortening until coarse crumbs form. Stir in the water, 1 tablespoon at a time, until you are able to form the dough into a ball.

On a floured sheet of waxed paper or countertop, roll out the dough to approximately ¼ inch thick.

To make the filling, brush the melted butter over the entire pie crust. Sprinkle the brown sugar and cinnamon evenly across the top. Roll into a log.

Cut off the ends and discard. Cut the log into slices approximately ½ inch thick. Place the rounds onto the prepared baking sheet and bake for approximately 15 minutes, or until the rolls begin to turn the slightest brown and the cinnamon mixture gets bubbly.

Cookies, Candies & Treats

Bourbon and Brown-Sugar Pecan Ice Cream

MAKES 1 QUART ICE CREAM

FOR THE BROWN-SUGAR PECANS

1 cup shelled pecan pieces

2 tablespoons butter

1 tablespoon light brown sugar

1/4 teaspoon kosher salt

FOR THE BOURBON ICE CREAM

2 cups heavy cream

1 cup half-and-half

2 cups Dixie Crystals Extra Fine Granulated Pure Cane Sugar, or sugar of choice

3 tablespoons bourbon

2 tablespoons vanilla extract

There is no greater summertime treat than homemade ice cream, but when the flavor profiles of bourbon, pecans, and brown sugar are combined, it's a decadent, elevated treat.

Preheat the oven to 350 degrees F.

To make the brown-sugar pecans, place the pecans on a baking sheet and bake for approximately 10 minutes, or until they become fragrant. Remove from the oven.

In a small saucepan over low heat, melt the butter, then add the brown sugar and salt and whisk together until bubbly. Remove from the heat. Add the toasted pecans to the butter mixture and stir to coat. Let cool.

To make the bourbon ice cream, in large mixing bowl, whisk together the heavy cream, half-and-half, sugar, bourbon, and vanilla.

Pour the mixture into an ice-cream maker and prepare according to the manufacturer's instructions, churning approximately 25 minutes. Stir in the pecans and mix 1 to 2 minutes, until combined.

Enjoy immediately or store ice cream in a freezer-safe container for 2 to 4 hours or overnight for harder ice cream.

Cookies, Candies & Treats

Old-Fashioned Southern Pralines

2 tablespoons butter, plus more for buttering

1½ cups sugar

1½ cups packed light brown sugar

⅛ teaspoon salt

3 tablespoons dark corn syrup

1 cup evaporated milk

1 teaspoon vanilla extract

1½ cups pecan halves, chopped, plus more for topping

DATING BACK TO THE 1750S, pralines were first made by the French with almonds and white sugar. The Creoles of New Orleans soon found a superior alternative, using pecans and brown sugar instead. Today, pralines are considered a staple of Southern candies.

Arguably the most Southern of candies, pecan-filled pralines are crunchy, creamy, and perfectly sweet, making them absolutely irresistible.

Butter the sides of a heavy 2-quart saucepan. Put the sugar, brown sugar, salt, corn syrup, milk, and butter in the pan. Over medium heat, stir the mixture constantly with a wooden spoon until the sugars have dissolved and the mixture comes to a boil. Continue to cook to a soft ball stage, approximately 236 degrees F on a candy thermometer. Remove from the heat and allow to cool for 10 minutes.

Add the vanilla and pecans, and beat with a wooden spoon by hand for 2 minutes or until the candy is slightly thick and begins to lose its shininess. Quickly drop heaping tablespoons onto waxed paper. Press extra pecan halves in the center of each candy.

Buckeyes

MAKES 12 COOKIES

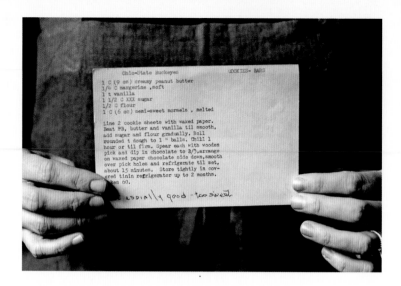

½ cup peanut butter

½ cup butter, room temperature

½ teaspoon vanilla extract

3½ cups powdered sugar

1 cup chocolate chips

1 tablespoon shortening

THIS RECIPE CAME straight from my stack of heirloom family recipe cards from my grandmother's collection. Apparently, it wasn't one of her favorites, based on the note she handwrote on the recipe card: "Not especially good—too sweet." I must disagree with her, but I love the sentiment and the fact that she made them with us each Christmas despite not loving them herself.

Most of my favorite treats combine peanut butter and chocolate. Always a part of our Christmas cookie baking assortment, these Buckeyes are a recipe I could eat every day to satisfy my sweet tooth.

Line a baking sheet with parchment paper and set aside.

In a stand mixer on medium speed, mix together the peanut butter, butter, and vanilla until combined and fluffy. Beat in the powdered sugar and combine until the dough is firm and with no lumps. Using a tablespoon, scoop the dough and roll into 12 balls. Evenly space the balls on the prepared baking sheet and place in the refrigerator for about 30 minutes.

In a microwave-safe bowl, combine the chocolate chips and shortening. Microwave the mixture in 30-second intervals until it is melted. Stir so that mixture is smooth and fully combined. Remove the baking sheet from the refrigerator. Using a toothpick, dip each peanut-butter ball into the chocolate mixture and return to the baking sheet. Refrigerate for 30 minutes before serving. If there are any leftovers, store them in the refrigerator.

Granny's Caramel Pecan Turtles

MAKES 16 TURTLES

32 whole pecans, shelled and halved

16 individual caramel squares

2 cups dark-chocolate melting wafers

WE HAVE FOND MEMORIES of using a pecan roller and picking up pecans off the ground with Granny beneath the trees in the pasture at the farm. Even late in life, she was a hard worker and would fill buckets full of pecans, and even crack and pick them herself. She'd have her freezer filled with pecans, ready to make batches and batches of this family-favorite recipe once the holidays came around.

This recipe comes from my husband's grandmother's collection. They were such a favorite with him and his siblings that she'd make them each a candy tin full during the holidays. They'd hide them from one another so no one could sneak someone else's turtles.

Line a baking sheet with waxed paper. Place 4 pecan halves on the baking sheet in the shape of a cross to create the base of the turtle. Repeat until all the pecans have been used.

In a microwave-safe bowl, melt the caramels in the microwave. Carefully drizzle a spoonful of caramel on the center of each pecan cross and flatten it down, being careful as the caramel may be hot. Repeat for all pecan groupings.

Once the caramel has been applied to each grouping of pecans, melt the chocolate via the same method and spoon a dollop on each turtle to complete the turtle's shell. Allow them to firm up, then indulge.

Sea Salt Caramel Sauce

½ cup sugar

1 tablespoon water

2 tablespoons unsalted butter

¼ cup heavy cream

¼ teaspoon sea salt

1 teaspoon vanilla extract

This caramel sauce makes a delicious topping for your favorite ice cream, brownie, or other sweet treat. Packaged in a Mason jar, it also makes a wonderful food gift for a friend or family member.

In a small saucepan over medium heat, combine the sugar and water together and bring the mixture to a boil. Once the sugar has dissolved, reduce the heat to a simmer.

Add the butter and whisk until combined. Let the mixture simmer for about 5 minutes, until it turns a deep brown color. Remove the pan from the heat and gently whisk in the cream until it is completely combined. Whisk in the salt and vanilla.

Carefully pour the sauce into a heatproof jar. Let cool before serving.

Grandma's Chocolate Fudge Sauce

MAKES ABOUT 1 CUP

⅓ cup unsalted butter

3 squares unsweetened chocolate

⅔ cup sugar

⅛ teaspoon kosher salt

1 (6-ounce) can evaporated milk

1 teaspoon vanilla extract

⅛ teaspoon almond extract

This is one of my very favorite recipes to make in a big batch. I love to give it in jars to friends and neighbors along with a pint of vanilla bean ice cream.

In a heavy saucepan over medium heat, melt the butter and chocolate, stirring constantly.

Remove from the heat and stir in the sugar and salt to form a thick mixture. Slowly add the evaporated milk, blending well.

Return to low heat and, cook, stirring constantly for 4 minutes.

Remove from the heat and add the vanilla and almond extracts. Cool to room temperature and enjoy over ice cream, or bottle and keep refrigerated.

Homemade Vanilla Buttercream Frosting

MAKES 2½ CUPS

1 cup butter, softened

4 cups powdered sugar

2 to 4 tablespoons heavy cream

1 teaspoon vanilla

Using stand mixer with the paddle attachment on medium speed, beat the butter for 2 minutes. Gradually add in the powdered sugar, 2 tablespoons of cream, and the vanilla into the butter on low speed. Increase to medium speed and beat for an additional 2 minutes.

Check for a spreadable consistency and add a bit more cream as needed. Use immediately to frost a cake or cupcakes, or cover and store in the refrigerator for up to 1 week.

Chocolate Buttercream Frosting

MAKES 4 CUPS

3 cups powdered sugar

3/4 cup unsweetened cocoa

1/2 cup butter, room temperature

4 tablespoons heavy cream, divided

1 teaspoon vanilla extract

This frosting recipe is super quick and easy to make and is a must-master in your recipe arsenal. Homemade chocolate frosting really does taste so much better than store-bought.

In a large bowl, sift the sugar and cocoa together. In another large bowl, combine 1 cup of the sugar mixture with the butter and 1 tablespoon cream, beating with a hand mixer until smooth. Add another cup of the sugar mixture and another tablespoon of cream, beating well. Continue until all ingredients are combined and the frosting is fluffy. Beat in the vanilla.

Cream Cheese Frosting

MAKES 2 CUPS

1 (8-ounce) package cream cheese

1/2 cup unsalted butter

2 teaspoons vanilla extract

4 cups powdered sugar

Everyone has their favorite treats when it comes to the classics, and a good old basic Cream Cheese Frosting is certainly at the top of my list. I mean, if I'm being honest, cream cheese is good in just about anything.

In a large bowl, use a hand mixer to beat together the cream cheese, butter, and vanilla. Add the powdered sugar gradually, 1/2 cup at a time, and continue to beat until fully incorporated.

 NOTE: Pairs wonderfully with Perfect Carrot Cake (page 172) or Red Velvet Cake (page 183).

Vanilla-Almond Glaze

MAKES ABOUT 1 CUP

1½ cups powdered sugar

½ cup milk

2 teaspoons vanilla extract

1 teaspoon almond extract

Made with powdered sugar, this simple glaze makes a great alternative to a thicker frosting for cinnamon rolls, pound cake, sugar cookies, and more. The addition of the almond flavor gives it a subtle richness.

In a small bowl, stir the powdered sugar with a fork to remove any lumps. Slowly stir in the milk, just a little at a time, to reach desired consistency. You may not end up using all of the milk. Add the vanilla and almond extracts, and more milk as needed. Stir until the mixture is a smooth, pourable glaze.

Royal Icing

MAKES ABOUT 3½ CUPS

4 cups sifted powdered sugar

3 tablespoons meringue powder

9 tablespoons water plus more as needed, room temperature

Gel food coloring, optional

NOTE: Royal icing takes about 2 hours to set completely. If you need it to dry faster, once your cookies are iced, place them in the refrigerator to help speed up the process.

Royal Icing is known for its crisp, white color and thick consistency that makes it the perfect decorative icing for beautiful and creative cookies.

Using a hand mixer or stand mixer with a whisk attachment on high speed, beat the powdered sugar, meringue powder, and water together for 5 to 7 minutes. When lifting the whisk out, the icing should drizzle down from the whisk in about 10 seconds. If the consistency is too thick, add 1 teaspoon of water at a time to smooth it out. If it's too thin, add a little more powdered sugar. If you'd like to color the icing for decorating, batch into smaller bowls, add gel food coloring, and stir to combine.

Homemade Whipped Cream

MAKES ABOUT 2 CUPS

1 cup cold heavy cream

2 tablespoons sugar

1 teaspoon vanilla extract

You know I love all things homemade, but some things are definitely worth the extra time and effort even more than others. Homemade Whipped Cream is one of them.

In a medium bowl using a hand mixer with the whisk attachment on medium-low speed, beat the cream, sugar, and vanilla together for 30 seconds, until well combined.

Beat on high speed until stiff peaks form, approximately 3 to 4 minutes; do not overbeat.

NOTES: I personally love my whipped cream on the less-sweet side, because I'm usually adding it to an already sweet dessert. I typically add closer to 1 tablespoon sugar than the 2 tablespoons specified here.

Also, there is some preference on using granulated sugar versus powdered sugar to sweeten homemade whipped cream. I was always taught using granulated sugar, but when making it in larger batches, it can get a little textured and you may want to stick to powdered sugar in such cases.

Praline Ice Cream Topping

MAKES ABOUT 3 CUPS

½ cup unsalted butter

1 cup packed light brown sugar

½ cup coarsely chopped pecans

2¼ cups cornflakes

Vanilla ice cream, for serving

It's easy to make this topping, which features a pantry-staple cereal you may already have on hand. Sweet, crispy, and nutty— it's everything and more to complement vanilla ice cream.

In a heavy-bottom saucepan over medium-high heat, bring the butter and brown sugar to a boil and cook for 2 minutes, stirring continuously.

Remove from the heat and stir in the pecans and cornflakes, tossing with a fork to fully coat. Serve warm over a scoop of vanilla ice cream.

NOTE: My mom loved cornflakes cereal for breakfast and always had a box on hand as a pantry staple. Creating or curating recipes that you can make on a whim with ingredients you already have on hand enables you to look prepared and always offer up an option when impromptu guests pop over.

PIES
&
CAKES

⋅—◦—⋅

There is just something so
nostalgic about baking
to me. It's romantic and a
time-honored skill
where the details count.
In my way of thinking,
everyone must learn
the art of baking from
scratch, so here we are.

Nana's Pie Crust

MAKES 2 (9-INCH) PIE CRUSTS

1½ cups all-purpose flour, plus
more for flouring

¾ cup shortening

Dash of salt

5 tablespoons cold water

My great-grandmother's recipe for a tried-and-true pie crust.
Add this recipe to your lineup.

In a medium bowl, mix the flour, salt, and shortening with
a pastry blender or fork until the mixture resembles small
pebbles. Stir in the water and turn the dough onto waxed paper.
Shape into two balls and refrigerate for 15 minutes. Turn onto
a lightly floured surface and roll out each dough ball into a
12-inch-round circle, perfect for fitting a 9-inch pie plate. The
dough will be about ⅛ inch thick. Move quickly so as to keep
the dough cold without too much handwork.

Buttermilk Pie

SERVES 8

½ recipe Nana's Pie Crust (page 164), prepared and rolled out

3 large eggs

1¼ cups sugar

2 tablespoons all-purpose flour

½ cup butter, melted

1 cup Made-from-Scratch Buttermilk (page 211) or buttermilk of choice

1 teaspoon vanilla extract

1 tablespoon lemon zest

1 tablespoon lemon juice

Pinch of salt

What is more all-American than a good old slice of pie? This sweet and simple Buttermilk Pie will become your next favorite Southern dessert. It may sound a little weird, but I promise you'll love the custard-like texture.

Preheat the oven to 350 degrees F.

Line a 9-inch pie plate with the pie crust and ensure the dough is pressed into the edges.

In a large bowl, mix together the eggs, sugar, flour, butter, buttermilk, vanilla, lemon zest, lemon juice, and salt until well combined.

Pour the mixture into the unbaked pie crust and bake for 45 to 50 minutes, until the pie is set and golden brown. Remove from the oven and allow to cool prior to slicing. Store in the refrigerator.

Frozen Key Lime Pie

SERVES 8

FOR THE CRUST

2 1/2 cups graham cracker crumbs

3 tablespoons unsalted butter, melted

2 teaspoons ground cinnamon

1 teaspoon powdered sugar

1/2 teaspoon nutmeg

FOR THE FILLING

1 (14-ounce) can sweetened condensed milk

1 teaspoon Key lime zest

1/2 cup Key lime juice

2 large eggs, separated

4 tablespoons sugar

1 Key lime, sliced, for garnishing

If I had a top-five list of my all-time favorite desserts, I think Frozen Key Lime Pie would be at the very top. Not just any Key lime pie will do—I love our family recipe the best. I think that's just the way it goes when it comes to recipes you've grown up enjoying through the years.

To make the crust, in a medium bowl, combine the graham cracker crumbs, melted butter, cinnamon, powdered sugar, and nutmeg. Mix well and spoon into the bottom of a 9-inch pie plate, reserving approximately 1/4 cup of crumb mixture for the garnish. With the back of the spoon, press crumbs evenly onto the bottom and sides of pie plate; set aside.

To make the filling, in large bowl, stir together the condensed milk, lime zest, lime juice, and egg yolks until well blended.

In a separate bowl, using a hand mixer, beat the egg whites until almost stiff enough to hold a peak. Add the sugar gradually and continue beating until stiff and glossy. Fold the egg whites into the filling mixture.

Spoon the filling into the graham cracker crust, spreading evenly to fill the pie plate. Garnish with the reserved crumb mixture and lime slices. Freeze for at least 1 hour before serving.

MY GRANDPARENTS LIVED in South Florida for many years and had a small Key lime tree right outside their front door. We would go out and gather the teeny little limes right off their tree and give them to my grandma. Then we'd walk across the street on the shell-filled, sandy path to the beach while she stayed at the house to make a Key lime pie for us to enjoy after dinner.

 NOTE: Not everyone serves their Key lime pie frozen, but in our family, this makes all the difference and is so refreshing on a hot summer day.

Rustic Blueberry Galettes

SERVES 8

FOR THE CRUST

2½ cups all-purpose flour, plus more for flouring

1 tablespoon sugar

1 teaspoon kosher salt

1 cup cold, unsalted butter

½ cup cold Made-from-Scratch Buttermilk (page 211) or buttermilk of choice

FOR THE FILLING

⅓ cup sugar

2 tablespoons cornstarch

Zest of 1 lemon

1 pound fresh blueberries, washed and patted dry

1 large egg

¼ cup sanding sugar

It doesn't get much more satisfying than incorporating fresh fruit into a pastry. I just love this blueberry version, but don't shy away from using your favorite seasonal fruit in this recipe.

To make the crust, in a large bowl, stir together the flour, sugar, and salt. Cut the cold butter into cubes, add to the flour mixture, and combine with a pastry blender or fork until the mixture resembles small pebbles.

Dump out the mixture on a floured surface and use a rolling pin to combine the butter evenly throughout the flour mixture. Work quickly and try not to use your hands to keep the butter as cold as possible. Return the dough to the bowl, and create a well in the center.

Add the buttermilk, using a wooden spoon to combine. The mixture should be on the dry side. Wrap in waxed paper and refrigerate for at least 1 hour, but up to overnight, to chill.

Preheat the oven to 400 degrees F.

To make the filling, in a medium bowl, combine the sugar, cornstarch, and lemon zest. Add the blueberries to the mixture and toss to coat.

Using a rolling pin, roll out the dough into 8 (3-inch) circles about ¼ inch thick. Remember they don't have to be perfect—this is supposed to be a simple and rustic dessert. Transfer the dough circles onto a well-greased baking sheet.

—❖ **HIGHLIGHTS** ❖—

What is a galette? A term for a pastry topped with filling where the edges are roughly folded over and baked into a rustic treat. Galettes are a fantastic pastry to make because they are so easy.

Spoon the coated blueberries into the center of the dough circles and then fold the edges of the dough up and toward the middle of the galettes so the blueberries are contained, pinching together the sides if needed.

In a small bowl, whisk the egg. Brush the edges of the dough with the egg wash. Generously sprinkle the sanding sugar around the surface of the dough.

Bake for 15 to 18 minutes, or until the crust is golden brown and the blueberry filling is bubbling. The dessert is best served warm.

Calypso Pie

SERVES 8 TO 10

18 Oreo cookies, crushed

¼ cup butter, melted, plus ⅓ cup butter

3 squares unsweetened chocolate

⅔ cup sugar

⅛ teaspoon salt

⅔ cup evaporated milk

1 teaspoon vanilla extract

⅛ teaspoon almond extract

1 quart coffee ice cream

1 cup heavy cream

3 tablespoons powdered sugar

1 cup chopped pecans

There are few things I love more than a delicious pie. Whether savory or sweet, a pie is something I find hard to turn down, and I always love finding new recipes. This Calypso Pie recipe comes from my aunt's kitchen, and it's one I cherish making—it is a tradition that I whip up this pie for Christmas dinner dessert every year. It makes the sweetest ending to a wonderful day full of family and celebration.

In a large bowl, mix the crushed cookies (cream filling included) with the melted butter. Press into 10-inch pie plate and chill in the refrigerator.

In a small saucepan over medium-low heat, melt the chocolate and the remaining ⅓ cup butter. Remove from the heat and stir in the sugar and salt. Gradually add the evaporated milk, blending well. Cook over low heat, stirring constantly, for about 4 minutes. Remove from the heat and stir in the vanilla and almond extracts. Cool to room temperature.

While the pie crust and chocolate sauce thoroughly cool, set out the ice cream to soften slightly. Fill the pie crust with the softened ice cream and put in the freezer until the ice cream is firm again.

In a large bowl, using a hand mixer, beat the heavy cream until it just holds a peak. Beat in the powdered sugar.

Remove the pie from the freezer and spread the chocolate sauce over ice cream layer, and then top with whipped cream and sprinkle with pecans. Store in the freezer until ready to serve. Remove from the freezer and let set a few minutes before serving.

Wild Strawberry Shortcakes

SERVES 6

FOR THE STRAWBERRIES

4 cups quartered strawberries

1 to 2 tablespoons sugar

FOR THE SHORTCAKE

2 1/3 cups Bisquick

1/2 cup milk

3 tablespoons sugar

3 tablespoons butter, melted

Homemade Whipped Cream
(page 160)

Mint sprigs, for garnishing

This recipe for Wild Strawberry Shortcakes, welcomes warm weather with open arms with its sweet taste, fresh ingredients, and vibrant colors. The "wild" comes not from the strawberries, but instead from the sprigs of fresh mint pulled from my garden that we use to top it with.

Preheat the oven to 425 degrees F. Grease a baking sheet and set aside.

In a large bowl, toss the strawberries with sugar and set aside.

To make the shortcake, in a medium bowl, mix the Bisquick, milk, sugar, and butter together until a soft dough forms. Drop 6 equal-size scoops of dough onto the prepared baking sheet. Bake for 10 minutes, until golden brown. Remove from the baking sheet and assemble the strawberry shortcakes while warm.

To serve, place a single shortcake onto a plate or in a bowl, and top with two spoonfuls of strawberries and a dollop of whipped cream. Garnish with fresh mint.

Perfect Carrot Cake

SERVES 8 TO 12

3/4 cup coconut oil, melted, plus more for greasing

2 cups all-purpose flour, plus more for flouring

1 cup sugar

3/4 cup packed dark brown sugar

4 large eggs

2 teaspoons vanilla extract

1 teaspoon baking soda

2 teaspoons baking powder

2 teaspoons kosher salt

2 teaspoons ground cinnamon

1/2 teaspoon ground nutmeg

2 1/2 cups freshly grated carrots

1 1/4 cups chopped pecans, divided

1/2 cup plump raisins

Cream Cheese Frosting (page 157)

Anytime we can get away with eating our vegetables and having a dessert at the same time is a win/win, right? Some people shudder at the idea of carrot cake, but let me tell you—this recipe just might win them over.

Preheat the oven to 350 degrees F.

Grease and flour 2 (9-inch) round cake pans and set aside.

Using a stand mixer, combine the coconut oil, sugar, and brown sugar until well mixed. Beat in the eggs and vanilla until smooth. On medium speed, slowly begin adding the flour, 1/2 cup at a time. Add the baking soda, baking powder, salt, cinnamon, and nutmeg and combine.

Fold the grated carrots, 1 cup pecans, and raisins into the cake batter by hand until thoroughly mixed. Pour the cake batter evenly into the prepared cake pans and bake for 25 to 30 minutes, or until a toothpick inserted into the center of the cake comes out clean. Allow the cakes to cool completely before removing from the pans.

Stack and frost the cakes with Cream Cheese Frosting. Top with the remaining 1/4 cup pecans.

Made-from-Scratch Chocolate Cake

SERVES 8 TO 12

2 cups all-purpose flour, plus more for flouring

2 cups packed light brown sugar

½ cup butter

2 large eggs, separated

½ cup cocoa powder

½ cup hot water

1 teaspoon baking powder

1 teaspoon salt

1 teaspoon baking soda

1 teaspoon ground cinnamon

½ cup sour milk (see Note)

1 teaspoon vanilla extract

Chocolate Buttercream Frosting (page 157)

Mom always made our birthday cakes from scratch. This chocolate cake has an incredibly moist center and is topped with the most delicious Chocolate Buttercream Frosting. It's sure to become a favorite in your family.

Preheat the oven to 350 degrees F. Grease and flour 2 (9-inch) round cake pans and set aside.

In a large bowl, using a hand mixer, cream the brown sugar and butter together, and then add the egg yolks. Stir in the cocoa powder and hot water, and let cool.

In a medium bowl, combine the flour, baking powder, salt, baking soda, and cinnamon. Add the dry ingredients to butter mixture alternately with the sour milk. Stir the vanilla into the mixture.

In a separate bowl using a hand mixer, beat the egg whites until stiff. Fold the egg whites into batter. Pour the batter into the prepared pans and bake for 35 to 40 minutes or until a toothpick inserted into the center of the cake comes out clean.

Allow the cakes to cool completely, then remove from the pans. Stack and frost cakes with Chocolate Buttercream Frosting.

NOTE: What is sour milk? My first guess was buttermilk, but that's not necessarily the case. A vintage ingredient you may find in old recipes, sour milk is literally milk that has soured, and thus has a tart or tangy taste. For this recipe, use buttermilk or ½ cup milk with ½ tablespoon vinegar or lemon juice stirred into it.

Fluffy Coconut Cake

3 cups all-purpose flour

1½ teaspoons baking powder

½ teaspoon salt

2 cups sugar

¾ cup unsalted butter, softened

¼ cup vegetable oil

6 large eggs, separated, room temperature (save 4 of the egg yolks for another use)

½ teaspoon vanilla extract

1 teaspoon coconut extract

1⅓ cups canned coconut milk, room temperature

⅛ teaspoon cream of tartar

Homemade Vanilla Buttercream Frosting (page 156)

1 (7-ounce) bag coconut flakes, for decorating

To me coconut and Easter just go hand in hand, but this recipe is worth making for any special occasion.

Preheat the oven to 350 degrees F. Grease 2 (9-inch) round cake pans.

In a large bowl, combine the flour, baking powder, and salt and whisk for about 30 seconds.

In a stand mixer with the paddle attachment, mix together the sugar, butter, and oil on medium speed until well combined. Slowly add in 2 egg yolks, 1 at a time. Mix in the vanilla and coconut extracts.

Make sure the coconut milk is well shaken. Working in three separate batches, beginning and ending with the flour mixture, add the flour mixture and the coconut milk alternately to the creamed butter. Add ⅓ of the flour mixture, then ½ of the coconut milk, and so on, mixing until just combined after each addition. If you don't have the paddle attachment that scrapes the sides of the bowl, stop the mixer and use a rubber spatula to scrape the sides and bottom occasionally.

In a separate mixing bowl, using an electric hand mixer, whip the 6 egg whites with the cream of tartar on medium-high speed until stiff (but not dry) peaks form. Using a rubber spatula, carefully fold ⅓ of the egg whites into the cake batter at a time and fold until just combined after each addition. Be careful not to overmix, which will deflate the egg whites.

Divide the batter between the prepared cake pans, spreading evenly. Bake 19 to 22 minutes, or until a toothpick inserted into the center of the cake comes out clean.

Allow the cakes to cool in the pans for 10 minutes before removing and completely cooling on wire racks. Once the cakes are cooled, use a knife to even the tops out to a smooth, level surface.

Spread the buttercream frosting on the top of one of the cakes. Stack the other cake on top and frost the top of it. Then frost the sides of the stacked cakes. To finish, sprinkle the coconut flakes around and on top of the cake. You may need to gently press the sides to get the coconut to stick.

Hummingbird Cake

SERVES 8 TO 12

3 cups all-purpose flour, plus more for flouring

2 cups sugar

1 teaspoon salt

1 teaspoon baking soda

1 teaspoon ground cinnamon

3 large eggs, beaten

1½ cups vegetable oil

1½ teaspoons vanilla extract

1 (8-ounce) can crushed pineapple

2 cups chopped ripe bananas (about 3 bananas)

1 cup toasted, chopped pecans, plus more for garnish

Cream Cheese Frosting (page 157)

This cake will be the star of the show, with its moist layers topped with Cream Cheese Frosting and toasted pecans.

Preheat the oven to 350 degrees F. Grease and flour 3 (9-inch) round cake pans and set aside.

In a large bowl, whisk together the flour, sugar, salt, baking soda, and cinnamon. Add the eggs and oil, stirring until the dry ingredients are moistened. Stir in the vanilla, pineapple with juices, bananas, and toasted pecans.

Divide the batter evenly between the prepared pans.

Bake for 25 to 30 minutes, or until a toothpick inserted into center of cake comes out clean. Cool in the pans for 10 minutes, then transfer to wire racks and cool completely, about 1 hour.

Stack and frost the cakes and top with chopped pecans for garnish.

THE ORIGIN OF THIS CAKE'S NAME ISN'T QUITE CLEAR, but it's been said it has to do with its sweet and fruity flavor, something that nectar-loving hummingbirds would be sure to enjoy. Reminiscent of a tropical vacation, it makes the perfect summer dessert. The addition of decadent frosting and toasted pecans make it even more irresistible.

Lemon and Sour Cream Pound Cake

1¼ cups unsalted butter, softened, plus more for greasing

3 cups flour, plus more for flouring

2 teaspoon vanilla extract

¼ teaspoon salt

2 teaspoons lemon juice

2¾ cups sugar

1 cup sour cream

6 large eggs

½ teaspoon baking soda

Vanilla-Almond Glaze (page 158)

Zest of 1 lemon, for topping

This pound cake has such a dense and moist texture that it will keep everyone wanting another slice. The hint of fresh lemon juice gives it just the right amount of zest, and sour cream makes it extra moist.

Preheat the oven to 350 degrees F. Grease and flour a loaf or Bundt pan and set aside.

In a large bowl, mix together the butter, vanilla, salt, lemon juice, and sugar. Add the sour cream and stir to combine, then add the eggs and stir to combine.

In a medium bowl, whisk together the flour and baking soda. Add this to the butter mixture, thoroughly combining the mixture.

Pour the batter into the prepared pan. Bake for 45 to 55 minutes. The cake is done when a toothpick or knife inserted in the center comes out clean.

Let the cake cool for about 30 minutes. Top with icing and lemon zest before serving.

Red Velvet Cake

SERVES 8 TO 12

½ cup unsalted butter, softened, plus more for greasing

2½ cups all-purpose flour, plus more for flouring

1¾ cups sugar

1 teaspoon baking soda

½ teaspoon salt

1 tablespoon unsweetened cocoa powder

1¼ cups canola or vegetable oil

3 large eggs, separated, room temperature

1 teaspoon distilled white vinegar

2 tablespoons vanilla extract

1 cup Made-from-Scratch Buttermilk (page 211) or buttermilk of choice, room temperature

1 to 2 tablespoons liquid red food coloring

Cream Cheese Frosting (page 157)

We love making this chocolate-cake-in-disguise for birthdays and special occasions in our house. And, it pairs just perfectly with our Cream Cheese Frosting.

Preheat the oven to 350 degrees F. Grease and flour 2 (9-inch) round cake pans and set aside

In a large bowl, mix together the flour, sugar, baking soda, salt, and cocoa powder. Using a stand mixer on medium-high speed, beat the butter and sugar together until fully combined. Add the oil, egg yolks, vinegar, and vanilla and beat on high for an additional 2 minutes.

Next, add in dry ingredients, alternating in three batches with the buttermilk until the batter is smooth. Add the food coloring to your desired shade.

In a medium bowl, use a hand mixer on medium-high speed to beat the egg whites until stiff peaks form, and fold into the cake batter.

Pour the batter evenly into the prepared pans and bake for approximately 30 minutes. The cake is done when a toothpick inserted in the center of the cake comes out clean.

Allow the cakes to cool completely in pans before removing them. Stack the cakes and frost with Cream Cheese Frosting.

CLASSIC COCKTAILS & DRINKS

·•—•·

Having a good arsenal of
classic cocktails in your rotation
is essential for entertaining.
We love to have a stocked bar,
a garden that helps with garnishes,
and a selection of seasonal
spirits to celebrate the moment.

Spiced Apple Cider

MAKES 2 QUARTS

2 teaspoons whole cloves

1 unpeeled apple of choice, cut in half

2 quarts apple juice

½ cup packed brown sugar

1 small, unpeeled orange, cut in ¼-inch slices

2 cinnamon sticks

½ teaspoon nutmeg

½ teaspoon allspice

I love the smell of apple cider cooking on my stovetop. The aroma of sweet apples and fall spices is my favorite during the cold months.

Push the cloves into all sides of the apple.

In a Dutch oven or large saucepan over medium heat, heat the apple juice. When it is hot, slowly stir in the brown sugar until it dissolves. Add the apple with cloves, orange slices, cinnamon sticks, nutmeg, and allspice. Reduce the heat and let the mixture simmer for about 20 minutes, occasionally gently stirring.

Remove the apple, orange, and any other whole ingredients. Serve hot in your favorite mug.

NOTE: This recipe is also great made in a slow cooker. For Halloween, I'll often have a pot simmering when friends drop by while trick-or-treating. It's an easy way to warm up and guests can serve themselves.

Bourbon Slush

SERVES 6 TO 8

2 cups hot brewed tea of choice

1 (6-ounce) can frozen orange juice concentrate, thawed

⅓ cup sugar

1 cup bourbon

⅓ cup lemon juice concentrate

Mint sprigs or cocktail cherries, for garnishing, optional

This recipe was passed down to me from my grandmother's stack of recipe cards. It has been cooling people down on warm days through multiple generations.

In a freezer-safe container such as a 9 x 13-inch baking pan, combine the tea, orange juice concentrate, and sugar. Stir until the sugar dissolves. Stir in the bourbon and lemon juice concentrate and then freeze for several hours, depending on the size of the pan.

About 1 hour before serving, remove from the freezer and let it thaw a tad until slightly slushy. Take a fork and scrape it out of the pan. Spoon the slush into cocktail glasses and serve. Garnish if you wish with a sprig of fresh mint or cocktail cherry.

NOTE: For a classic take on this recipe, include a drizzle of grenadine with a cocktail cherry to top it off. I'm not a big fan of red in general, so I typically garnish with mint. I was glad to see Grandma's actual recipe didn't call for grenadine or a maraschino cherry either.

Elderflower and Prosecco Cocktail

MAKES 1 COCKTAIL

Prosecco, chilled

St-Germain elderflower liqueur

Sprig of fresh herb, such as thyme or basil, for garnishing

This light and refreshing cocktail is just what the doctor ordered for your spring hosting and entertaining.

Fill your favorite serving glass about ¾ full with the Prosecco. Add just a splash of St-Germain to really make the flavors pop. Garnish with a fresh herb sprig and enjoy.

Fall Bourbon Cocktail with a Cinnamon-Sugar Rim

MAKES 1 COCKTAIL

8 ounces apple cider, plus more for dipping the glass

2 ounces bourbon

1½ teaspoons maple syrup

Ice

1 teaspoon ground cinnamon

1 tablespoon sugar

Dried apple crisps, for garnishing

Rosemary sprig, for garnishing

Cinnamon stick, for garnishing

This fall apple cider cocktail balances warm notes of cinnamon with the sweet, familiar taste of apple cider. Serve for peak fall entertaining.

In a cocktail shaker, combine the apple cider, bourbon, and maple syrup with ice and shake until well combined.

Mix the ground cinnamon and sugar in a shallow bowl or plate. Dip a cocktail glass into a little bit of apple cider to wet the rim, then press into the cinnamon-sugar mixture to coat.

Place ice cubes into the sugar-rimmed glass, pour in the cocktail mixture, and garnish with apple crisps, a rosemary sprig, and a cinnamon stick.

Classic Cocktails & Drinks

Gin and Tonic

MAKES 1 COCKTAIL

2 ounces gin

4 ounces tonic water

Ice

2 lime wedges, for garnishing

With herbal and citrus notes from the gin of your choice, this gin and tonic is one I gravitate toward, especially during the summer. The G & T is such a classic cocktail for the young and old alike.

In a cocktail glass of your choice, pour the gin and tonic water over ice. Squeeze lime wedges into the drink and mix, or leave them on the rim of the glass.

Hand-Squeezed Lemonade

MAKES 1 GALLON

2 cups sugar

2 cups water

2 cups freshly squeezed lemon juice, 8 to 10 large lemons

Ice, for serving

Fresh lemon slices or mint sprigs, for garnishing, optional

NOTE: You can use club soda instead of water for a more carbonated beverage, or choose to make a flavored simple syrup (like lavender or mint) for a fancier take on your homemade lemonade.

A timeless summer beverage staple is an ice-cold pitcher of fresh lemonade. My kids love having lemonade stands, as did I when I was growing up. It's a wonderful, nostalgic tradition that will stay with you.

In a large saucepan over medium-low heat, heat the sugar and water, stirring continuously until the sugar is dissolved to make a simple syrup. Allow to cool completely.

In a gallon-size pitcher, combine the simple syrup and the lemon juice and stir until well mixed. Top with cold water to fill the pitcher and stir. Serve over ice, garnished with lemon slices or mint sprigs as desired.

Classic Cocktails & Drinks

Spicy Bloody Mary

1 lime slice

Kosher salt, for the rim

2 ounces vodka

½ cup tomato juice

3 drops hot sauce

4 drops Worcestershire sauce

½ tablespoon horseradish

Salt, to taste

Freshly ground black pepper, to taste

1 lemon slice

Ice

Bacon, shrimp, olives, pickled okra, and celery, for garnishing

It's customizable, it's a drink, it's an appetizer, and it's so delicious. I know a few people who would consider it a great way to get their vegetables in too. Just a few of the top reasons this cocktail takes the cake.

Slide the lime slice around the rim of a cocktail glass to give it a nice coating. Using a plate lined with the kosher salt, press the rim of the glass in the salt to coat.

In a cocktail shaker, combine the vodka, tomato juice, hot sauce, Worcestershire sauce, and horseradish with the ice and shake until combined. Season with salt and pepper. Strain the mixture into the salt-rimmed glass. Squeeze lemon over the top. Garnish as desired.

YOU CAN REALLY STAY AS CLASSIC OR GO AS CRAZY as you'd like for the garnishes. The classic option would be to stick with a celery stalk, a few olives, and a pickle. But if you're feeling adventurous you can try cocktail shrimp, bacon, pickled okra, pickled green beans, tiny ears of corn, or just about anything else. You can even get a little fancy with the salt rim and add chili powder to your mix before dipping the glass.

I like a little kick to my Bloody Mary, but I can't do anything overly spicy. Just like my mom and grandmother, I add a heavy hand of horseradish, with a dash of hot sauce. I use Crystal Hot Sauce because it's that perfect amount of hot sauce flavor without all the heat that tends to go along with it.

The Old-Florida Cocktail

MAKES 1 COCKTAIL

Ice, crushed or cubes

1½ to 2 ounces tequila blanco

¾ ounce (about 2 squeezes) fresh Key lime juice

Topo Chico, or other sparkling water

1 Key lime wedge, for garnishing

We developed this signature cocktail as part of the launch campaign for our Palmetto pattern. The drink, inspired by old Florida, is a cross between a Texas ranch water cocktail and a margarita. The tartness of fresh Key lime juice and the smokiness of tequila makes a refreshing and easy beverage everyone is sure to love.

In a lowball glass, combine the ice, tequila, Key lime juice, and enough Topo Chico to fill the glass. Mix together with spoon. Add a lime wedge for a garnish.

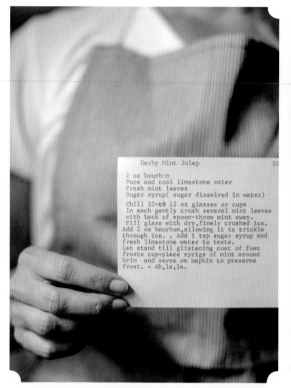

Derby Mint Julep

2 oz bourbon
Pure and cool limestone water
Fresh mint leaves
Sugar syrup(sugar dissolved in water)

Chill 10-to 12 oz glasses or cups
In each gently crush several mint leaves
with back of spoon-throw mint away.
Fill glass with dry,finely crushed ice.
Add 2 oz bourbon,allowing it to trickle
through ice. . Add 1 tsp sugar syrup and
fresh limestone water to taste.
Let stand till glistening coat of foam
frosts cup-place sprigs of mint around
brim and serve on napkin to preserve
frost. - Ah,la,la.

Classic Cocktails & Drinks

Derby Mint Julep

MAKES 1 COCKTAIL

3 mint sprigs, for muddling and garnish

½ ounce Mint Simple Syrup (below)

2½ ounces bourbon

Splash of cold water

Crushed ice

1 teaspoon powdered sugar

Mint juleps are best known for being the signature drink of the Kentucky Derby. Keep the tradition alive and add this cocktail to your rotation.

Pluck the leaves from 2 sprigs of mint and place in the bottom of a large jar. Add the Mint Simple Syrup and, using a muddler or the end of a wooden spoon or rolling pin, muddle together the mint leaves with the syrup, bourbon, and water. Fill a glass with crushed ice and pour mixture over top. Sift the powdered sugar on top and garnish with the remaining sprig of mint.

Mint Simple Syrup

MAKES 1 CUP

1 cup sugar

1 cup water

1 cup fresh mint sprigs

This Mint Simple Syrup truly is simple. I love adding it to a cocktail or glass of lemonade for fresh flavor.

In a small saucepan over medium heat, bring the sugar, water, and mint to a boil. Simmer for 2 minutes, and then pour the liquid into a clear, heatproof jar through a mesh strainer. Be sure to push on the mint leaves and any solids in order to wring out all liquid. This stores for up to 2 weeks in the refrigerator.

 NOTE: You can substitute any herb you might have growing in abundance, like rosemary or lavender, in this recipe. You can also make and keep a few small jars on hand in your refrigerator when your herb garden is at its peak. It's a great way to preserve the flavor and also fills your house with the most wonderful aroma.

Dehydrated Oranges

Growing up in Florida, one of the most nostalgic tastes and smells to me is a fresh, juicy orange. I always am sure to have a Mason jar of dehydrated oranges on hand in my fridge for cocktails, garnishing, and décor. I usually dehydrate oranges in batches, making many at a time, so that I can stock up and store them for later use.

TO MAKE IN THE DEHYDRATOR

Slice the oranges (as many as will fit in your dehydrator) about ¼ inch thick, with the peel.

Lay out the orange slices on the stackable dehydrator trays. Set to 130 degrees F and let the orange slices dehydrate for about 2 days. Depending on how dried out you want them to be, and how thickly you sliced the rounds, check for more or less time. I usually consider them finished when they have a translucent quality.

TO MAKE IN THE OVEN

Preheat the oven to 200 degrees F.

Line baking sheets with parchment paper and set aside.

Slice the oranges about ¼ inch thick. Lay out the orange slices in a single layer on the prepared baking sheets. Bake for about 2½ hours, or until translucent.

TO STORE

When the orange slices are finished dehydrating, store them in glass jars.

After being dehydrated, these oranges last in the refrigerator for a substantial amount of time. My research says that you can keep dehydrated oranges around for up to two years, but mine never make it that long before getting used up in cocktails, recipes, or decorations.

Classic Cocktails & Drinks

Classic Cocktails & Drinks

Mojito Punch Bowl

SERVES 8 TO 10

1 bundle mint leaves, plus more for garnishing

2 limes, sliced, plus more for garnishing

1 cup lime juice

1 cup Mint Simple Syrup (page 195)

2 cups white rum

2 cups chilled club soda

Ice, for serving

Not only is this drink a hit at parties, but it makes for a beautiful centerpiece in a glass punch bowl on the table or kitchen counter.

In a punch bowl, combine mint leaves, sliced limes, lime juice, simple syrup, rum, and club soda. Using a muddler or end of a wooden spoon or rolling pin, muddle the mint leaves with the other ingredients. Garnish bowl with lime slices and fresh mint leaves. Serve over ice.

Old-Fashioned

MAKES 1 COCKTAIL

½ teaspoon sugar

3 dashes Angostura bitters

1 teaspoon water

2 ounces bourbon

Ice

Dehydrated Oranges (page 196), for garnishing

Amerena cherry, for garnishing

An ode to dads everywhere, the Old-Fashioned is the quint-essential drink to serve in celebration of Father's Day. It's my husband's favorite.

Place the sugar in the bottom of an Old-Fashioned glass. Add the Angostura bitters and water; muddle together until the sugar is dissolved. Stir in the bourbon and ice.

Garnish with a Dehydrated Orange and a cherry.

NOTE: A cocktail-loving friend of ours gave us the special twist of adding a Dehydrated Orange to an Old-Fashioned. You can also smoke your cocktail glass to add a deeper level of flavors for the true Old-Fashioned connoisseur.

Back Porch Sun Tea

½ to 1 cup sugar, to taste

8 cups boiling water

5 to 6 tea bags, of choice

Ice, for serving

I always remember a jar of tea sitting out on our back porch, brewing in the summer sun. Learn how to make Back Porch Sun Tea with a just a few steps. It will soon become one of your favorite summer activities.

In a ½-gallon Mason jar or pitcher, pour ½ to 1 cup of sugar, depending on how sweet you like your tea.

Fill the jar or pitcher nearly full to the neck with the boiling water. Using a wooden spoon or spurtle, mix until the sugar fully dissolves.

Add 5 or 6 tea bags, making sure to hang the strings and tags over the edge of the jar so they don't fall in completely.

Give it another swirl with the spoon and allow the tea to steep for at least 2 hours in full sunlight. Bring inside and discard the tea bags, mixing again with wooden spoon until fully combined. You'll notice the color of the tea is now much darker.

Pour over a glass of ice and enjoy!

Screw the lid on the jar and store any remaining tea in the refrigerator.

—❖• **HIGHLIGHTS** •❖—

A "spurtle" is a wooden Scottish kitchen tool dating back from the fifteenth century. Spurtles are great for stirring soups, stews, broths, and tea.

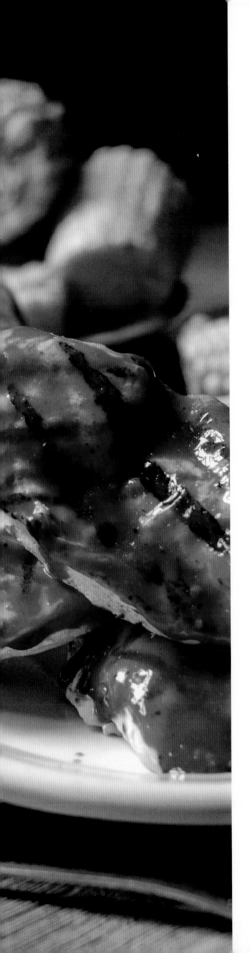

SAUCES, CONDIMENTS & MORE

·:——:·

The unsung heroes are the
accoutrements that add flavor,
personality, and pack a big punch
to any dish. These are some
classics you should master—
you'll be surprised at how much
better a simple homemade sauce
can be when everyone else is
used to packaged varieties,
it can make a dish.

Sauces, Condiments & More

BBQ Sauce

MAKES ABOUT 1 CUP

1 cup ketchup

2 tablespoons apple-cider vinegar

1 garlic clove, minced, or 1 tablespoon garlic powder

Salt, to taste

Freshly ground black pepper, to taste

This classic BBQ Sauce recipe is straight out of my grandmother's collection of typewriter recipe cards. It's a quick and easy sauce for ribs or pulled meat. I love a tangier, vinegar-based sauce.

In a medium bowl, combine the ketchup, vinegar, garlic, salt, and pepper together to make the sauce.

Serve it right away or store in an airtight container or jar in the refrigerator for up to two weeks.

 NOTE: You can adjust the ingredient amounts to taste. Try adding rosemary, sweet basil, or oregano for different flavor profiles.

Homemade Mayo

MAKES 2 CUPS

1 cup extra-virgin olive oil

1 tablespoon white vinegar

2 egg yolks

1 tablespoon dry mustard

1 tablespoon lemon juice

In my opinion, mayo makes everything taste so much better, and it's even better when it's homemade.

In a medium bowl or wide-mouth Mason jar, combine the olive oil, vinegar, egg yolks, mustard, and lemon juice.

With a handheld blender, blend the mixture together until it reaches a creamy consistency. This usually takes about 30 seconds. Spread on your favorite sandwich, add to salads or meat dishes, and enjoy.

Alabama White Sauce

MAKES ABOUT 3 CUPS

2 cups Homemade Mayo
(page 205)

½ cup apple-cider vinegar

3 tablespoons lemon juice

1 tablespoon Worcestershire
sauce

2 teaspoons freshly ground
black pepper

1 teaspoon cayenne pepper

1 to 2 teaspoons horseradish

Salt, to taste

*This recipe for Alabama White Sauce has just the right amount
of tang and flavor for a summer barbecue. It's a Southern staple
to add to your grilling routine as the perfect alternative to your
traditional BBQ sauce.*

In a medium bowl, combine the mayonnaise, vinegar, lemon
juice, Worcestershire sauce, black pepper, cayenne pepper,
horseradish, and salt. Cover and chill before serving

 NOTE: You can modify this recipe a bit if needed. For example, add a little more apple-cider vinegar for a thinner
sauce with a bit more bite, or a little more cayenne pepper for added spice. Also, don't just think meats when
you make up a batch. This white sauce is delicious on everything from veggies to corn on the cob to coleslaw.

Pickled Red Onions

MAKES ABOUT 4 CUPS

2 red onions, thinly sliced

2 garlic cloves

1 teaspoon peppercorns

1 teaspoon mustard seeds

2 cups water

2 cups white vinegar

⅓ cup sugar

2 tablespoons sea salt

Add some zing to your favorite salads, sandwiches, and tacos with these homemade Pickled Red Onions. A great garnish to have on hand in your fridge, they are as tasty as they are beautiful.

Thinly slice the red onions and stuff the slices into 2 (8-ounce) Mason jars. Equally divide the garlic, peppercorns, and mustard seeds between the jars as well.

In a small saucepan over medium heat, heat the water, vinegar, sugar, and salt until the sugar is completely dissolved. Let the mixture cool, then pour over the onions in the Mason jars.

Tightly screw on the lids and let cool to room temperature. Once cooled, store in the refrigerator. Let them set overnight, until the color is pink and onions are tender. They keep in the refrigerator for up to 2 weeks.

Sauces, Condiments & More

Fig Tree Jam

MAKES 2 PINTS

2 pounds fresh figs

1 cup sugar

Juice of 1 lemon

½ teaspoon almond extract

¼ cup water

Jellies and jams are some of those things I can't resist picking up at a general store or when I'm traveling. I tend to go for the reds—a classic strawberry or raspberry will do—and the chunkier and fruitier the better in my book. But I love this jam because when my fig tree is in bloom and producing fruit, there is so much at once and I can never use it all. Creating a batch of this jam makes me feel like I'm making good use of the beautiful tree in our yard.

Remove the stems from the figs and cut the fruit into quarters. In a medium saucepan, toss the figs, sugar, lemon juice, and almond extract to evenly coat. Cook over medium heat, stirring frequently, until the sugar is completely dissolved.

Turn the heat to low, add the water, and simmer for approximately 30 minutes, stirring occasionally, until the fig mixture is soft and the liquid begin to thicken.

Turn off the heat and spoon the jam into 2 heatproof pint jars. Place the lids on the jars and allow to cool to room temperature. Refrigerate the jam after cooling. It will keep for about 1 week.

Sauces, Condiments & More

209

Made-from-Scratch Buttermilk

MAKES ABOUT 1 CUP

4 cups heavy cream

Buttermilk is a staple throughout this cookbook. To elevate your dishes that much more, use this recipe for making buttermilk at home. It's easier than you may think and a great way to make a little when a recipe calls for it and you don't have any on hand.

In a stand mixer with a whisk attachment on medium speed, beat the heavy cream for approximately 10 minutes, or until a butter solid begins to form a ball with liquid remaining at the bottom of the bowl.

The ball of solid that remains is butter (see page 212). Remove the butter solids and pour the liquid buttermilk through a fine-mesh strainer or cheesecloth to capture any remaining butter solids. Pour it directly into a jar or container and use immediately or refrigerate for later. Store for approximately 3 to 5 days in the refrigerator.

NOTE: If you're in a pinch and don't have heavy cream readily available, you can use this shortcut to make buttermilk: Use 1 cup of regular milk and add 1 tablespoon of lemon juice or white vinegar. Let it rest for approximately 5 minutes, or until it begins to slightly curdle and have a buttermilk-like texture and thickness.

—❖ **HIGHLIGHTS** ❖—

Buttermilk comes from the leftovers of churned butter, letting nothing go to waste, which is always important in my kitchen. You could call this a two-in-one recipe. For more information on making and using Homemade Butter, see page 212.

Homemade Butter

4 cups heavy cream

¼ teaspoon kosher salt, or to taste

Arguably the most popular ingredient in any Southern dish, here's how you can easily make butter at home.

In a stand mixer with a whisk attachment on medium speed, mix heavy cream, approximately 10 minutes.

As the cream begins to thicken, it becomes whipped cream. As it mixes longer, it will begin to solidify and clump together, separating itself into butter solids and buttermilk liquid. Once this occurs, turn off the mixer.

Gather the butter solids into a flour-sack towel or cheesecloth. Pour the buttermilk through a fine-mesh strainer or cheesecloth to capture any remaining butter solids. Pour it directly into a little jar or container and save the buttermilk to use later (see page 211).

Squeeze the remaining buttermilk out of the butter solids, wringing out as much as possible. Try to handle it as quickly as possible as the butter will begin to soften and melt.

In a medium bowl, wash the butter in a bath of cold water to remove any remaining buttermilk. Buttermilk residue will make the butter sour more quickly, become rancid, and not keep as long. The water in the bowl will be cloudy for several baths; continue until it runs clear.

Sprinkle the salt on the butter and knead it in. Roll the butter into a log and wrap in waxed paper. Store the butter in the refrigerator for up to 1 week.

Honey Butter

½ cup unsalted butter, room
temperature

2 tablespoons milk

2 teaspoons honey

1 teaspoon kosher salt

Try this on a homemade biscuit or with chicken. It's great for both sweet and savory foods.

In a medium bowl, using a hand mixer on low speed, beat the butter and milk 1 to 2 minutes, until blended. Beat on medium speed for another 2 to 3 minutes, until whipped and fluffy.

Add the honey and salt and fold in until combined. Serve immediately; store any remaining butter in a sealed container in the refrigerator for up to 5 days.

Fresh Herb Butter

½ cup unsalted butter, room
temperature

3 rosemary sprigs

1 bundle fresh chives

1 teaspoon minced garlic

Kosher salt, to taste

This creamy spread tastes excellent atop almost any dish you can imagine—cornbread, steak, homemade biscuits, and more.

In a small bowl, stir the butter with a large spoon until creamy. On a chopping board, pull off needles from the rosemary, add the chives into the pile, and chop the herbs into small pieces.

Add the chopped herbs, garlic, and salt to the butter and stir to combine. Spoon the mixture onto a small sheet of waxed paper and roll into a ball or log, twisting the edges of the waxed paper to seal. Place in refrigerator until chilled; store for approximately 3 to 5 days.

Sauces, Condiments & More

ACKNOWLEDGMENTS

This book was many years (and many generations) in the making, and I want to sincerely thank and acknowledge those who have supported me along the way, allowing me to celebrate the continuation and techniques of made-from-scratch cooking and baking, and the sharing of family recipes.

First, to my husband, Shane, who supports every crazy idea without question, you are my biggest cheerleader and are always there for me. I love you and this life we have built. To my children, Wyatt, Sawyer, and Waylon, who I love with all my heart and who are always on hand to model or taste-test any recipe. I am beyond thankful for our family.

To my grandmother, Cele, who was the matriarch of our family and who inspired my love of entertaining, made-from-scratch cooking, and my business, Heirloomed. To my mother, Judy, who is a tireless supporter, and who always made-from-scratch every birthday cake, family dinner, and sweet treat in our home while I was growing up. To my father, James, who gave me my lifelong love of learning, passion for history, and respect for our family roots. To my sister, Courtney, who has always been my greatest companion and friend. To my stepmom, Dawala, who inspired my passion for antiques and the techniques of cooking in a Southern kitchen. To my in-laws, Johnny and Cecilia, who are constant supporters and who always put the gathering of family first.

To more family members who have inspired me in the kitchen and many of whom were kind enough to lend me their own family recipes to include for you in this book, Aunt Jo, Aunt Carol, Tina, Nana, Granny, and beyond.

To my many friends, girlfriends, and supper-club ladies, who are always there through thick and thin, good times and bad. Gathering with family and great friends will always be the greatest treat in life.

To my friend and longtime photographer, Heidi Harris, who is insanely talented and whom I couldn't have done this without, who has set the visual tone for our brand from the very beginning.

To my right-hand gal, Kelsey Thibadeau, for her constant support, creative thinking, organization, and for keeping every wheel spinning in our studio each and every day. To Holly Parker and Anne Henley Walker for getting this project off the ground, from organizing photos to writing recipe copy. To Jessica Berinato, Amanda Wilbanks, Emily Raffield, and all my countless entrepreneur friends who have grown up alongside me and my business, lending a hand or advice along the way.

To Michelle Branson and the amazing team at Gibbs Smith for believing in our book concept and always putting my vision and our brand at the forefront of the process. I am truly thankful for the opportunity to put so many years of recipes and my passion out into the world.

INDEX

ABOUT THE AUTHOR

Ashley Schoenith is a self-proclaimed old soul on a mission to keep family recipes and heirlooms around for future generations. From a young age, she always had an affinity for history, made-from-scratch cooking, a love of craftsmanship, a fondness for vintage details, and an obsession with preserving things from the past.

Schoenith is a home cook who learned to cook, bake, and entertain from an early age by years spent together in the kitchen with family. She is a textile designer and founder of the brand Heirloomed. Born and raised in Tallahassee, Florida, she graduated from the University of Georgia and now resides in Atlanta with her husband Shane and three children, Wyatt, Sawyer, and Waylon.

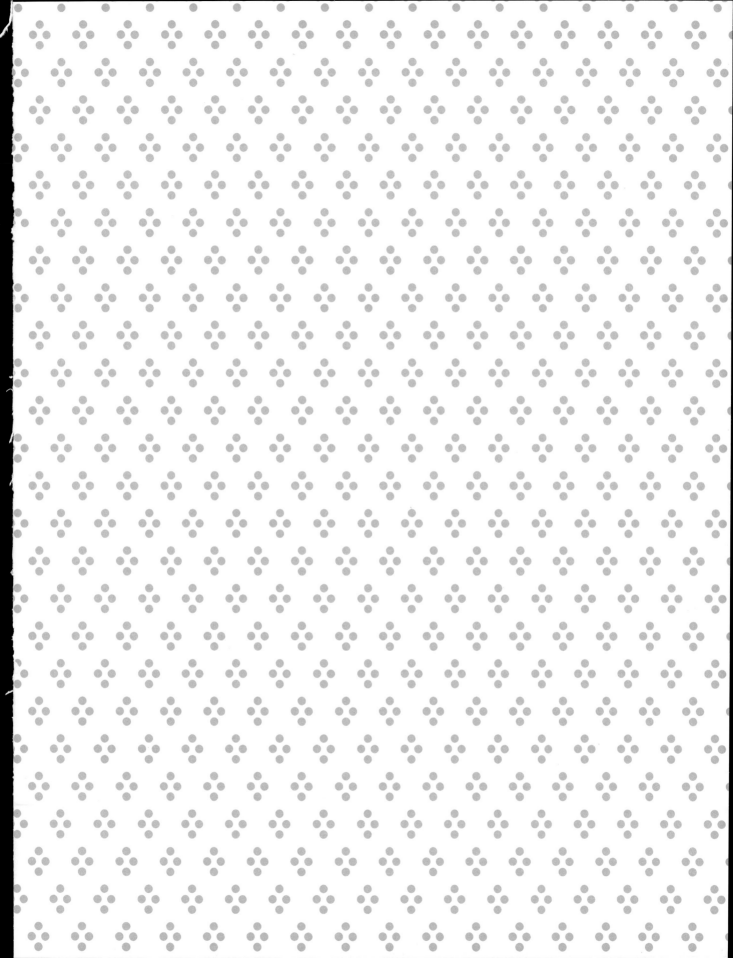

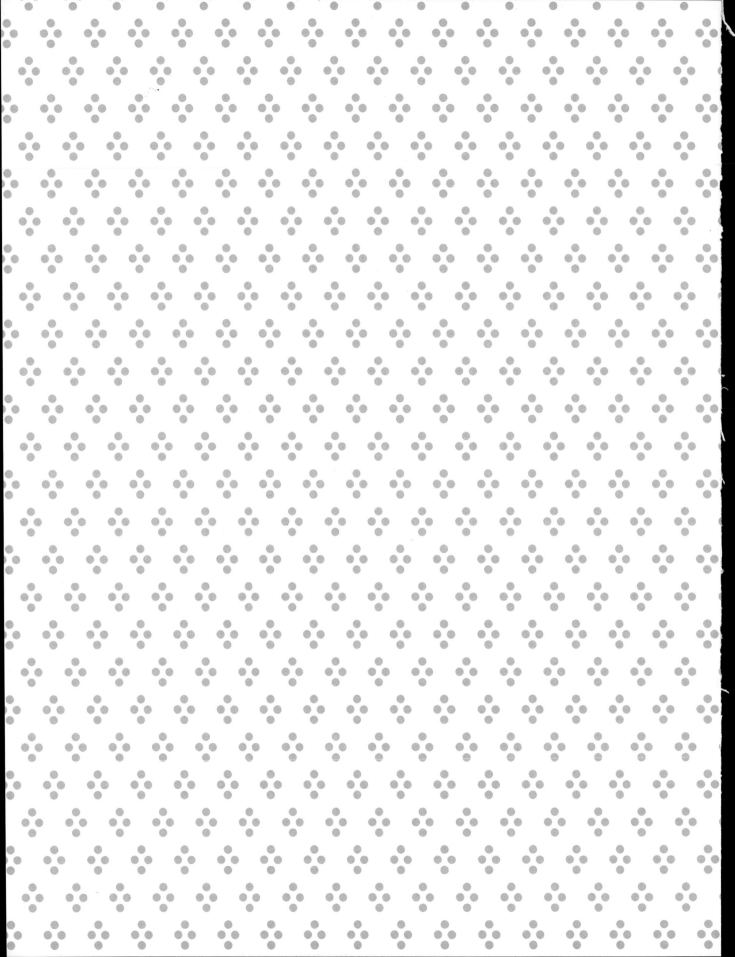